"The women of Genesis are fascinating, yet the narratives are terse. Jill Eileen Smith imagines what may have happened between the lines, and it causes us to ponder. How did the fall affect Adam and Eve's marriage? And what could we learn from this so that our marriages are better? Why did Lot's wife look back after God's clear warning? And how could we learn from this so that instead of our hearts turning to stone, they turn to flesh? You'll be both educated and entertained by *When Life Doesn't Match Your Dreams*."

Dee Brestin, author of *The Friendships of Women* and *He Calls You Beautiful*

"Steady and strong. Relatable and real. In *When Life Doesn't Match Your Dreams*, Jill Eileen Smith paints a portrait of the woman's heart with deep longings, thoughtful questions, and a gentle pen. Through the imagined lens of notable Old Testament women—imperfect heroines of the faith—we see a God-breathed story emerge, even from faults and failures, letdowns and pain. In the space between their stories and the concerns facing women in our world today, we find a bridge back to Him . . . and ourselves. This book has incredible heart—a drumbeat of God's enduring love for those we call mothers and daughters, sisters and friends."

Kristy Cambron, bestselling author of the Hidden Masterpiece novels and the Verse Mapping Bible studies

D1114218

Books by Jill Eileen Smith

THE WIVES OF KING DAVID

Michal

Abigail

Bathsheba

WIVES OF THE PATRIARCHS

Sarai

Rebekah

Rachel

THE LOVES OF KING SOLOMON (ebook series)

The Desert Princess

The Shepherdess

Daughter of the Nile

The Queen of Sheba

DAUGHTERS OF THE PROMISED LAND

The Crimson Cord

The Prophetess

Redeeming Grace

A Passionate Hope

When Life Doesn't Match Your Dreams

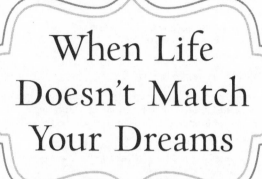

When Life Doesn't Match Your Dreams

*H*ope *for* Today
from 12 Women *of the* Bible

JILL EILEEN SMITH

Revell
a division of Baker Publishing Group
Grand Rapids, Michigan

© 2019 by Jill E. Smith

Published by Revell
a division of Baker Publishing Group
PO Box 6287, Grand Rapids, MI 49516-6287
www.revellbooks.com

Printed in the United States of America

Library of Congress Cataloging-in-Publication Data
Names: Smith, Jill Eileen, 1958– author.
Title: When life doesn't match your dreams : hope for today from 12 women of the Bible / Jill Eileen Smith.
Description: Grand Rapids, MI : Revell, [2019]
Identifiers: LCCN 2018027342 | ISBN 9780800728670 (pbk.)
Subjects: LCSH: Christian women—Religious life. | Women in the Bible—Biography.
Classification: LCC BV4527 .S65 2019 | DDC 220.9/2082—dc23
LC record available at https://lccn.loc.gov/2018027342

Published in association with Books & Such Literary Management, 5926 Sunhawk Dr., Santa Rosa, CA 95409, www.booksandsuch.com.

19 20 21 22 23 24 25   7 6 5 4 3 2 1

To every woman who has ever wished
her life could be different, better.
May you know without a doubt God loves you.
He can be trusted.
There is always hope in Him.

Contents

Introduction

I fell in love with the Bible when I was sixteen. Growing up in a Christian home, I'd been exposed to my mom and dad reading the Scriptures each day, and I tried to follow in their footsteps. But the Bible didn't really come *alive* for me until I read a biblical novel—*Two from Galilee* by Marjorie Holmes. When I closed the pages of that book, I thought, *These people were real!*

Thus started my journey into Bible study and reading every biblical novel I could find. But somewhere along the way, I discovered that what I wanted to read wasn't out there, so in the next phase of my journey I began to write the biblical novel I wanted to read—one about the life of King David.

The journey to writing well enough for publication took twenty years due to raising a family and the many other interruptions of life. But in 2009 my dream of publication came to fruition when Revell published *Michal*, book 1 in the Wives of King David series. Since then Revell has graciously worked with me to publish ten full-length novels and four novellas, with more to come. You could say I have seen my dreams come true.

So why would a biblical novelist want to write a nonfiction book on women of the Old Testament who *didn't* always see their dreams come true? Why pursue trust in God when life doesn't go the way we'd hoped, when it feels more like He's failed us?

The answer is that our journeys don't end with one goal reached. Life is full of twists and turns, and the roads we travel don't always lead to where we intended to go. Sometimes we are faced with choices we never wanted to make, or things are pushed upon us we didn't expect. Those are the moments our faith is most tested, and we have to decide whether we are going to believe that God has abandoned us or that He has never left our side and He has our best interests at heart.

I believe, from my years of studying the Scriptures for the novels I write, that these women of the Old Testament can teach us much about life's journey. They may have lived thousands of years before us, but the truth is, the human heart doesn't change with the passage of time. Only God can do such a miraculous work as changing a heart.

We are all at different places in life's journey, but if you are like me, you've hit a few bumps in the road, felt some of the joys dissipate and the hurts accentuate. When we can't see the dreams anymore, when life is more trial than triumph, that's when we can let our faith either come to a grinding halt or grow stronger.

I hope you will journey with me into the lives of these women and perhaps see trusting God from a new perspective, from the way they might have seen Him. If you have read my biblical novels, some of these women will be familiar to you, but you will get a different glimpse of them in these pages. I hope in the end that you and I together can grow stronger in our faith and *know* that God keeps His promises. He doesn't leave us or forsake us (Deut. 31:6; Heb. 13:5). And He is worthy of our trust, even in our darkest hours.

In His Grace,
Jill Eileen Smith

1

Eve

Will Life Ever Be Right Again?

(BASED ON GENESIS 3–4)

If I Were Eve

Day dawns, the sun's rays harsh on my face, so different from the feeling of warmth they once gave me. I dare to look heavenward for the briefest moment, but my eyes cannot linger. The beauty that once was, the ability to see light and hold it, has vanished. Everything changed the day we left the garden. Would I still be able to hold light's gaze if I could enter Eden once more? Could the Tree of Life turn time back and make everything right—as it used to be?

But no. I've known the answer to this endless, guilt-ridden question for months, even tried to approach the angels with the flaming swords a time or two, but they knew. And I could not even draw near.

Adam blames me. Before I even wake each morning, he leaves the shelter we were forced to build when the animals grew fearful of us. I won't see him again until evening, when he will expect me to have found enough for us to eat, while he fights with the earth to bring forth food from the seeds he has planted. He resents every briar and thistle and thorn that stops him. I know he misses the easy cultivation of the garden. Growth took little effort in Eden. Here, though there is beauty, it is flawed and clouded and dark.

And there is fear.

So much fear.

I wrap my arms about myself, the feel of the lamb's skin against mine still new, still awkward. Every touch of the skin brings me shame. And guilt. Unending guilt. Not only for my foolish choice but also for the precious lamb—one of the precocious beauties of the flock—that God chose and killed on our behalf.

I wish I could undo it. I wish I could go back and tell that evil being what I think of him now. I wish I had never followed his voice toward that tree.

I wish Adam had stopped me.

It doesn't matter that God held him most accountable. I feel the anger seething inside of him with every look my way. I was to complete him. I was to be one with him, but now he can barely look at me, let alone touch me. And our joyous conversations have been reduced to grunted orders and silence.

So much silence.

Tears threaten as I listen to that silence now. Oh, the birds still chirp and the lions roar in the distance. Owls hoot at night and beavers scamper near the rivers where I draw water. Otters play, though they do not allow me to pet them as they once did. We cannot speak to the creatures at all. Their languages are foreign to us now, and I see the fright in their eyes.

Fright and anger and silence and guilt.

And the worst of it? Adam is right. It is truly my fault.

Why did I listen to the serpent? I did not understand that a creature of the Creator could lie to me. I know now that a different enemy seduced me, enticed me to believe something that was not true. And it has changed us.

Oh to go back to what was! *Oh God, how I want to fix it, start over, make it right. But I can't even fix my relationship with the only other human on earth.*

Was God even listening?

How I miss our talks with God in the cool night breeze, when the tangy crispness of the air touched my tongue. When our hearts would beat in unison with His, a joyous rhythm at the sound of His footfalls among the soft grasses.

But God no longer visits us at night, and when I attempt conversation with Adam, his bitterness cuts like a flint knife.

Please love me again. But I do not ask it of him.

I am not sure Adam will ever forgive me. I'm not even sure I can forgive myself, though the Creator said He forgave us when He gave us the lamb's flesh to cover our shame. He said the lamb's blood allowed Him to forgive.

His forgiveness comes at too high a price. And I know that I do not deserve to walk freely when an innocent had to die in my place. It is too much. Adam cannot accept it and neither can I.

I've caused too much pain to ever feel free again.

In Our World

The house stands in stillness, my people have dispersed, and I walk about like something weighted has settled in my chest. Tears fall hard, and the cry of *why* plays like a mantra in my head. I feel lost and defeated, as though I have failed at so many things. Was I that kind of friend? Was I really so needy or thinking life was all about me? If I'd listened more, said less . . . if I could have foreseen . . . if I'd known . . . I walk back through my mind, trying to make sense of all that had happened that day.

What did I do to cause this? Did I cause this? Is it really my fault?

I'd like to say these kinds of memories are of one isolated incident, that most of my life has been free from misunderstandings and difficulties, but I don't write humor very well. We all know life isn't that simple. We all know that life will always carry waves of trouble on what should otherwise be a calm sea.

And trouble brought on by our own actions—that's hard to accept, isn't it? We can look in the mirror and see our reflection, but how much harder is it to look into our hearts and make an honest evaluation of ourselves? We often don't like what we see, so we ignore, deny, refocus, blame others, stay frantically busy, or do any number of things to keep from facing the person we have become. When bad things happen because of our own choices, it takes a lot of honesty and maturity to admit and agree with God that we are at fault. Or that we at least had a hand in it.

I don't say this to accuse or point fingers at anyone but myself. The Bible tells us that there is no one who does right (in God's eyes, by His standards)—not even one (Ps. 14:2–3). Later it says that all have sinned and fallen short of the glory of God (Rom. 3:23). All. That's me. That's each one of us.

To fall short is to miss the mark. It's to copy Eve's behavior because we now have the sin nature that our foreparents did not have in the beginning. We were not created to sin. We were created in God's perfect image.

But Eve's choice caused a seismic shift to cross all lines of humanity for every generation to come after her. When she blew it big-time, the consequences were unequaled. (The fault was Adam's too, but she gets a lot of the blame for it—after all, it was *her* idea to listen to the seducing words of the evil one.)

While we may not blow it in a way anywhere close to what Eve did, we still suffer consequences. We aren't likely to make a choice that's going to affect all of humanity for all time. But we can affect the lives of those who know us. And we can make choices that carry devastating effects.

I'm talking about broken interpersonal relationships.

You've seen it too, haven't you? How many people do you know with at least one family trial or crisis? How many friends have pulled away for reasons you don't understand?

It's not always our fault. It's not always our choice. While sometimes things happen unexpectedly and leave us reeling— as in the spouse or child who walks away or the abusive boss or the bullying "friend"—we face relationships that make life just plain hard.

Then there are those times when we see that reflection in the mirror and realize we really should not have said what we did. Have you been there? I have. I think of the times I've wanted to say some pretty harsh things to people who have hurt me. Most of the time I take those to God and journal my hurts and forgive. But there are those emotional times when I simply react and say things I regret. The worst part? I can't take back those words. I can't stuff them in a bottle and cap it and pretend they were never said. I can't erase the blackboard or make the other person forget. Good grief, even *I* can't forget, so why should they?

I can ask for forgiveness, but that doesn't mean the person I've offended will forgive. Sometimes relationships can be forgiven but not restored, and I think that is one of the biggest heartaches on earth. Lies, abuse, slander, malice, bitter words . . . all of these things break a relationship, perhaps even one that has been in place for a long time.

(Side note: If you are living in an abusive relationship, one that is physically and emotionally harmful to you or your children, get help. Don't allow yourself to be destroyed on the altar of good intentions. God does not ask us to live under the weight of abuse or danger when it is in our power to leave. That's not to say He can't heal and restore, but that won't happen until help is received and wanted. An abuser is not going to change without wanting to, and seeking the help he or she needs.)

Broken relationships are complicated and not always fixable—at least not by us. God can do anything, but we have to ask for His help and take it. Eve had a huge problem when she made her choice, but her choice was not to simply "be like God, knowing good and evil" (Gen. 3:5). What she was actually doing, and Adam with her, was breaking *their perfect relationship* with God. She didn't stop to think of this possible cost to them all, but that's what happened. Any choice that breaks a relationship is a choice that longs for a do-over even if we aren't aware of it. We know deep down we've blown it and we can't fix it, and it needs fixing.

But as we think about the horrific consequences of our own choices—sometimes selfish, sometimes forced upon us, sometimes simply deceived—we, like Eve, can't handle the blame. We can't deal with that kind of guilt, and we wonder if life will ever be right again. That's why Adam and Eve hid from God and tried to cover their nakedness.

Nobody wants to feel exposed, and when we do something we regret and people find out about it or it destroys a relationship, we feel shame. And unaccepted shame leads to anger because we hate feeling guilty, don't we? So we shift gears and point fingers.

Blame tends to go in cycles. First we might consider blaming ourselves, but when that hurts too much, we blame another person or our circumstances. *She could have explained it better. He didn't have to lash out that way. She should have done . . . He shouldn't have said . . .*

And then the questions shift.

Where was God when that near stranger verbally attacked me or my child suffered such hurt? Why didn't He stop that mistreatment that bordered on abuse from someone I called friend? Why didn't He stop me from reacting instead of reasoning?

I pull out my journal in times like these. My hand aches with the frantic writing as if I'm pacing the lines and spaces instead of a room. I don't understand. *Lord, why is it so hard to understand?* A sob bursts forth and I can't stop it. Tears drip onto the fresh ink, marring the lines as my vision blurs.

I don't handle this kind of heartache well. While I am quick to forgive, I have a terrible time understanding when others don't forgive me as easily. I second-guess myself. Question every word. Go over and over what was said or done. *God, how do I fix this?*

Have you been there? Experienced pain too real, too fresh? We find ourselves in the throes of pain and blame with every bad choice, even while surrounded by people who love us. Maybe those choices don't come very often. Hopefully we are blessed with a heart of kindness and treat others with love and respect. But I daresay we all have those moments, even if they only happen once, where we wish life would stop, rewind . . . *Where is the backspace key? I want to rewrite that scene.* But life isn't a story we're writing—well, some would say it is. Rather, God is writing our story, though we still have a will to do what we want. And those wants are what get us into trouble.

Sometimes my throat hurts from unshed tears, and I remember Martha's words to Jesus one long-ago day: "If you had been here, my brother would not have died" (John 11:21).

I see that I'm not the only one who tries to blame God when things don't go right. Adam did it, Mary and Martha did it, Jonah did it, and many more did it throughout the ages.

What mother among us hasn't wished she'd been more patient, not lost her temper, stopped being so busy so she could actually sit down and know her kids? Which one of us in our daily, hectic lives hasn't longed to erase the hurt in our daughter's eyes that haunts us hours, days, even years after the fact? Which one of us hasn't had at least one moment when we've looked at ourselves and wondered how we could turn against the very people we love the most? That sudden realization of "What have I done?" or wishing we could start a conversation over, removing every word that just came out of our mouth, hits like a fist in the gut.

We hurt each other all the time. We say something without thinking. We try to control our circumstances or our people, and we don't stop to recognize that control was never in our hands.

My thoughts wander again to Eve, to the perfection she knew from the day she drew her first breath. What did garden air taste like? Are the colors that shape our world now dull in comparison? Is the sky less brilliant? *Why did you eat the fruit?*

Life has a way of showing us that none of us is always right. Sometimes that makes us run from the truth. Sometimes that makes us blame someone else.

There was a time in my life when I went through a crisis of fear—maybe slightly similar to what Eve faced after Eden. This wasn't a blame issue—yet. It was a trust issue. Did I trust God enough to be honest with Him regarding my fears?

I wrestled with Him, faced many a sleepless night, and couldn't understand what was going on inside of me. Since I was pregnant at the time, I could have blamed it on hormones, but I know it was so much more.

Stacks of those tearstained journals line my shelves, pages splattered with questions and heart cries to God from that time in my life. *I'm so confused. Why is this happening? I can't sleep. How do I fix this? Oh Lord, will You forget me forever?*

This went on for months until one day I finally closed our bedroom door and cried out to God, this time in honesty. *I'm scared, Lord. I don't trust You with this.* And on it continued until I could finally admit to myself what God already knew.

When Eve took that fruit and gave it to Adam, she did a world of damage, and it has followed us to this day. When God walked in the garden and asked Adam and Eve where they were, it wasn't like He didn't know. And when they blamed each other, it wasn't like He didn't see the truth behind their justification.

In the same way, He understood my lack of trust, my blinding fear. And once I could admit that fear to Him in detail and give it to Him with open hands, He gladly took it. He freed me from fear's tyranny. I wasn't afraid of eternal things; I feared losing earthly things—losing those I loved.

Fear simply makes us cling too tightly to what isn't ours in the first place. Everything we have comes as a gift from our loving God. We get to enjoy these things for a time, but they do not belong to us. I needed to learn to let go. To open my tightly clenched fists. The truth is, sometimes that is a lesson I have to learn again and again.

I've had to learn to allow God to forgive my poor choices, whether others forgive me or not. And I have also learned that while I may point to Eve and tell you that she started the mess we are in, I cannot blame her either. I cannot blame the person who won't forgive my rash comment. I don't have the right to ask the questions God asked Adam and Eve, because I'm not Him. He alone knows our hearts, and if you know the end of their story, you know that even in His judgment of their sin, He offered mercy.

Of course, one lesson learned is simply one lesson. Life has a way of bringing other besetting sins to our minds. And while I may have conquered one type of fear, I've gone on to face a host of others. Or a host of other sins.

Today it might not be fear but pride. Or selfishness. Or lying. Or a weary sense of defeat. A multitude of things can persuade us to justify ourselves and ignore the truth that is causing us pain. But we can only ignore pain so long. Eventually, our hearts will reveal what we try to hide, and we will look in the mirror and see a woman who needs to feel whole again.

I believe that was Eve's greatest need after her fall from grace. To feel whole again. To find those relationships with God and with Adam restored. No, she couldn't undo her actions or fix something only God could fix, but she was God's child, and He loved her and made a way for her to be in communion with Him again. He even made her a promise of a Savior yet to come, to mend what she could not.

Eve may have stolen our ability to make perfect choices by disobeying the one command God had given to her and Adam. Ironically, some people think what she did was a good thing. In our twisted thinking, we don't realize that innocence is far better than the knowledge of evil. To know only good. To never face the pain this world has to offer. Why would she give that up?

Now instead of being born into a perfect world with minds that always make the best choice, we come flailing and crying into brokenness. And we grow up desperately trying to get back what was lost in Eden.

Eve plunged the world into darkness so deep that I don't think we will ever fully grasp it. We just keep reliving it. Just because we light a candle or flip a switch doesn't mean the darkness is gone. We've simply made the darkness a little more bearable.

Eve lived a long time after the garden—probably far longer than the time she had spent in its splendor. No doubt she grew used to the changes that took over the world, the darkness that penetrated her heart.

We all do, don't we? We've grown so used to the darkness that surrounds our world that we fail to realize God has something far better planned for us. We can't see the future except through eyes of faith, so we get used to flickering lights in the growing darkness. Sometimes we grow numb to it until something jars us into the realization that this isn't how it's meant to be.

I wonder if Eve grew so used to her surroundings, her new reality, that she began to think of evil as something that had always been. Until that awful day when she lost her son.

Imagine with Me

I look up from the grinding stone at the sound of screaming. One of my daughters draws close, running hard, her face crimson. She trips, falls to the ground, pushes up again, and lunges toward me.

"What's wrong?" My heart stops at the look of terror in her eyes.

And then I see him stumble toward me. Adam. Holding a bloodied cloak in his clenched fist, his face agony.

I force shaking legs to stand and stagger toward him. I cannot mistake the cloak for another's. *Abel!* My mind screams his name but my throat constricts, useless.

I pry the cloak out of Adam's hands. He releases his grip and falls to his knees. My perfect, masculine husband buries his face in his hands and weeps.

I hold Abel's cloak to my chest, and I weep with Adam long before I know the details, because I know by the blood and the absence of my son that he is dead.

It is not until hours later that I discover my firstborn has done the unthinkable. He has killed his brother.

Who can forgive him for such an act?

But it is then that I remember—I am as guilty as if my own hand had slain him. My guilt mingles with Cain's in Abel's blood, and I wonder if either of us will ever be forgiven.

From Regret to Freedom

There are some things in life that do seem unforgivable. Either we cannot forgive others or we cannot forgive ourselves. We don't believe God would forgive us, so we hide in the shadows of our own torment or in the bondage of our own blame.

Why, Lord? When?

> How long, O LORD? Will you forget me forever?
>   How long will you hide your face from me?
> How long must I take counsel in my soul
>   and have sorrow in my heart all the day?
>   (Ps. 13:1–2)

Can you relate to the psalmist's plea?

I'll be honest here. Although I've shared what Eve can teach us, as well as some of my own fears and regrets, I'm still learning to trust even after that day in my room and those openhanded prayers.

The details of our hurts don't matter so much as the fact that we have them. We blow it. We live with guilt and shame and become tangled in crippling bitterness and an unwillingness to forgive others or accept God's forgiveness of us. And we wonder if life will ever look different, be better.

How many times have I cried out to God to change my circumstances, or, if not, to give me grace to accept, to forgive—again?

I've been the brunt of others' hostility and I've dished out my own, sad to say. Broken, guilty people do that. Eve may have started it, but we do have a choice of whether or not we want to carry her burden. Just because we are born in sin with a penchant to blow it, to mess life up, doesn't mean we have to stay in that state.

If Eve had longed for a do-over, I think she and I would have been best friends, because I've been there. Have you felt the same? Wrestled with guilt? Wished you hadn't gotten out of bed that morning?

I was sorting through old papers the other day and came across something one of my kids had written, and it made me cry. Why hadn't I been more soft-spoken? More understanding? More patient? Why didn't I trust that God is God and He's big enough to handle what I cannot?

Maybe like Eve, I just wanted to experience a taste of life the way I thought it should be instead of the way God had created it. But small things turned into big things. Molehills grew into mountains. And the mountains grew so tall and fat that no one could climb over or go around them to reach the hurting person on the other side.

We are paralyzed by others' anger or our own fear of honesty. Like in the Old West standoff, either we hide behind the mountain or we face each other, guns drawn.

But weapons of any kind (and guilt is a weapon of the enemy) don't heal us. Weapons don't make us whole on the inside. Like Eve, we are only forgiven because God makes a way for us to have a relationship with Him. Eve didn't get to go back to those walks in the cool of night, but God didn't abandon her or Adam or their family or the generations that have come from the mother of all the living. God still spoke to them, just not on the same level. There was now a gap between them.

Yet it's in those gaps that we come to see our need of someone to bridge the chasm. Like with the Grand Canyon, we can't jump across, but if someone ever built a bridge, we could get to the other side.

Jesus built that bridge, though Eve didn't know Him yet. She knew only of the promise of His coming to undo the consequences of her overwhelming shame. He didn't leave her without hope. He overcame what she could not so we could be free of our own guilt and all that separates us from people and from God.

When life hits us so hard we want to hide, or go into overdrive and work ourselves into constant denial, or fall into a habit of escape or a pit of depression—which are all really symptoms of the same feelings—we need to know we can't change anything. But God can.

Eve had to eventually realize that she couldn't go back. She couldn't restore Abel's life. But Cain, who had killed him, could be forgiven. We can *all* be forgiven if we but ask.

One thing I've learned, even in those times when I've wrestled with guilt or hurt in a big way, is that I have to let the outcome be God's.

Sometimes we learn that lesson the hard way, as Adam and Eve did. But in the end, that hard lesson can lead to a place of trust. When life doesn't go the way we'd planned because of our own foolish or selfish choices, can we stop fearing the future and trust that God still knows how to work things for our good? When faced with the "can't go backs," can we allow a loving Father to lead us forward into freedom with something far better than we could imagine?

Ponder this

When guilt or hurt makes us feel like life will never again be the same, we have a God who says,

> *I have blotted out your transgressions like a cloud*
> *and your sins like mist;*
> *return to me, for I have redeemed you. (Isa. 44:22)*

We don't need a do-over when we have a God who redeems what we've lost. And when we trust Him, every stolen thing becomes a restored thing in His capable, loving hands.

Taking it further

1. Have you ever ruined a good relationship, even unintentionally? How did that make you feel?
2. When have you blamed others and refused to consider your own faults? Have you ever found it hard to accept God's forgiveness? Why or why not?
3. Are you afraid to trust God to fix what you can't? If so, why? Do you prayerfully give Him the problems that He is so good at healing? How have you tasted freedom?

2

Adah
(Noah's Wife)

Surviving a World Gone Crazy

(BASED ON GENESIS 6–9)

If I Were Noah's Wife

Birds sing a discordant note in the trees at the back of our land. We are surrounded by beauty, with every variety of foliage in bloom and fruit hanging as though begging to be picked. The garden, though once difficult to tend due to thorns and thistles, has grown so quickly the girls and I can barely get things harvested and preserved fast enough.

Life has changed for us since Noah heard God speak and was told to build that ark, as he calls it, which takes up an entire field beside our home. While we are blessed with bounty, it has become necessary to guard our land from those who would loot us by night.

Sweat trickles along my brow, and I wipe it with my sleeve. Sela sat beneath the window and watched last night, ready to wake Shem in a heartbeat. But the quiet held, and she sleeps now while Keziah and Talitha help me work.

The sound of the mallet against the gopher wood rings with rhythmic consistency while male voices drift to us from the field. For now all remains as it should, but the mockers will come soon, and Noah will tell them again how they must repent and turn to God. He has been preaching for years, but not one among our neighbors or relatives pays him heed.

I glance at my two daughters-in-law and thank God they believe and they love my sons. I am blessed, I tell myself again and again, though a part of me grieves.

I stand from bending over the crate of radishes and cucumbers I have picked and rub the small of my back, looking closer at Keziah. Ham chose her after losing Naavah to the demigods. A shiver works through me at the memory.

"Ima!" Ham's hoarse voice had come from a distance, but his footfalls drew closer to the house. "Abba!" There were tears in his tone, and when he dropped to his knees in front of the door, he was clearly weeping. "They took her! I know they did. I can't find her anywhere."

"Calm down, my son. Who took whom? Come into the house and tell me." Noah's voice had the ability to soothe, but Ham would not listen.

"No! You must come with me to find her. We must get her back."

At this a weight settled in my middle as though I had swallowed a millstone. "You speak of Naavah."

"Of course I speak of Naavah. Why else would I be angry?" He gulped down a sob as his brothers came from working on the ark at the sound of his screams.

"What happened?" Shem's brow knit and his whole expression held pain. He knew. We all knew. But it would help Ham to tell us, even if we did not want to hear it. Did not want to believe it could happen, that God would allow us to be so touched by such evil.

Adonai, no! She was to marry our son. She was to come with us on the ark.

But one of the demigods had kidnapped Naavah, and there would be no rescue, no escape. She would be his until she bore his child, and if she pleased him she might bear another and another. But her life would not be her own from this day onward, for the demigods were brutal and stronger than two or three men combined, and taller than a man by half or more. A woman stood no chance against their desire.

I shiver again, recalling how Ham had spilled the tale. He and Naavah's father had searched, but when they'd heard her friends tell of the crazed man who had carried her off, Ham's legs turned to liquid and he lost all strength. A full hour had passed before he gained the ability to run home and tell us—in hopes that his father, by God's power, could bring her back.

I attempt to shake away the memory and stretch my aching back again. I turn toward the area where the men are working. It does no good to relive the violence. It continues to happen around us so often that the Nephilim, as the offspring of these unions are called, have begun to roam the land, especially that area designated as belonging to Cain.

Noah refuses to cross the line between Seth's land and Cain's, for even Seth's land has grown corrupt and violent and very few can be trusted. But Cain's descendants have built walls and towers and rule the people with a hostile grip.

A sigh lifts my chest as I slip in among the trees and watch the men, the memory of Ham's pain still playing in my mind. Naavah had been a beautiful girl, and Ham had fallen hard for her the moment he met her on a trip to town. Noah had been hesitant to approach her father, a descendent of Cain, but for the sake of Ham, who would have no other, he had gone. I still think of her parents and wonder how they feel about everything that happened to their only daughter.

A touch on my shoulder makes me turn to find that Sela has awakened from her rest. "Is everything going as expected?" She searches my face, and I know she wishes the work on the ark would progress more quickly.

"Noah has had to redo the areas where the crew sabotaged some of the planking. But there is still time." I glance at the sun. Noah claims that God has set a time for the work to be completed, that His Spirit will not always strive with men, but that time is not yet. "Our God is patient, my daughter. He waits to see if there will be repentance from any of our kinsmen or neighbors. Noah does not waste a moment trying to convince them."

Sela stands silent. At last she speaks. "I have tried desperately to convince my mother." She pauses, and I face her. "But she and my father and my brothers and sisters will not listen. They do not mind that I married Shem, but they think his family . . . that is, they think Noah is not in his right mind."

It is the most she has said to me of her family in years. Though we have talked of them, we have done so in superficial ways. We have invited them over, and they have listened to Noah attempt to convince them. They have laughed lightly at his insistence that the ark will one day be used and that anyone who wishes to survive the destruction of the world must be on it. They have politely changed the subject.

"You spoke to them recently then." I did not think she had the courage, for Sela is the quiet sort, but when tears fill her eyes, I pull her into my arms. "There, there."

"I waited, Ima Adah. I thought if I just gave them time . . . And then I tried to speak to my mother alone and I almost had her convinced. She told me she would speak to my abba that evening. But when I went back the next day, she told me to never speak of it again."

Tears fill my eyes as I see the pain in hers. What is there left to say? I have watched Noah practically beg his workers and some of our relatives to listen, but they turn their heads as if they have not heard. And the few women who will still speak to me at the market in town shut down my words at the slightest hint of any mention of judgment or the ark.

"My brother is getting married next month, and I am not invited," Sela says, interrupting my thoughts. "They do not wish to see me again."

And they likely won't. But I do not say so. "Perhaps things will change. Perhaps as we continue to pray, God will soften their hearts."

"The world has gone crazy, Ima Adah. I am afraid to walk the streets at night, even near our home here. I watch the gardens from the window, but I dare not step outside in the dark. Who knows if the Nephilim will cross the line between

Cain's land and Seth's? Even Seth's descendants are corrupt. I cannot get a decent price for anything I try to purchase, and no one will buy my work."

I place one arm around Sela's shoulders and walk her closer to the ark, which now stands above our heads. Yet the project is only half of the forty-five feet high that it will be once Noah finishes the work. "Soon there will be no need to sell anything, my daughter. In fact, we may be glad to have the extra items for all of the people who will change their minds and join us before it is too late."

In Our World

I grew up in a good Christian family. Everyone knew Jesus. My parents took us to church, read their Bibles daily, served others, and cared about people. They showed us what it meant to help others, to listen, to open their home when it wasn't convenient, and to be what it seemed a Christian should be. I learned early on to care about the souls of my friends and extended family.

Sometimes I didn't always go about witnessing in the most tactful way, as when I told a good friend in junior high school that if she didn't trust Jesus she was going to hell. We tend to be less blunt these days, but may I say that God works despite our tactful or tactless attempts to share His truth? That friend, by God's grace, knows Jesus today, which pretty much blows my mind every time I think about where we were then and where we are now. And we get to be forever friends because of Jesus!

(Side note: My friend has no memory of my words to her about Jesus and hell that long-ago day. It was not my witnessing that led her to Jesus. Jesus found her all by Himself. But it's pretty cool that He still wants us to share our faith with others. Who knows whether our prayers might play a role in someone else's faith journey?)

Sometimes, though, my boldness didn't have such an awesome outcome.

One day in that same junior high school, a teacher asked the class to write out their philosophy of life. I wrote of my faith in Jesus and how it shaped my life. (I was kind of known as a Jesus freak in those days. Probably still am!)

That teacher, however, wasn't very pro-Christian, so I wasn't surprised when he read my philosophy to the class and I heard a hint of disdain in his tone. I think he read it to embarrass me. And no one else in that class came to stand with me. They didn't want to be singled out either.

I wonder if Noah's wife felt a little like that. Did she witness to her friends the way Noah preached to his? We are only told that Noah was a preacher of righteousness. We actually don't even know his wife's name. I named her and her daughters-in-law for the purpose of this chapter. But I wonder, was her faith bold? Or did she just quietly work beside her family, doing what needed to be done? How did she view her world before God spoke to Noah and told him to build the ark? Surely she saw the violence and corruption. Life was far from perfect and probably a lot worse than it had been when she was a child.

Life is never as perfect as it seems to our innocent eyes.

She was thrust into Noah's call from God, and like it or not, she was living with a man who was building a giant ship in their yard. I have no trouble imagining the taunts. Can you?

I look around our world today and think, *Are we really any different?* If we've read the Genesis account and accepted the possibility of a worldwide flood, we'd like to know why, wouldn't we? Genesis 6:5–6 tells us, "The LORD saw how great the wickedness of the human race had become on the earth, and that every inclination of the thoughts of the human heart was only evil all the time. The LORD regretted that he had made human beings on the earth, and his heart was deeply troubled" (NIV). Noah's world was a far cry from the world God first called "good."

If you had told me back in my innocent years that my perfect Christian family would struggle with faith—that *I* would struggle with faith—I wouldn't have believed you. If you had told me that some of the Christians I looked up to and respected would let me down, or that those strong believers would fall short of what I was taught we should be, or that I would spend a lot of years wrestling with God and what I thought He should be, I'm not sure I could have handled the knowledge of what the future might hold for me personally.

Haven't we all seen it, though? Which one of us has not been touched by the chaos of our fallen world?

Violence. Corruption. Those are a couple of the things that got Sodom and Gomorrah into trouble. And though God didn't outright name immorality in Noah's day, the image of the "sons of God" having sex with the "daughters of man" (Gen. 6:2) pretty much gives that impression.

Immorality. Violence. Corruption. Sounds awfully familiar, doesn't it? We live in a world gone crazy.

Jesus told His disciples that in the last days before He returned, life would be as it was in the days of Noah. People would be going on with their lives and acting like things were just fine—even if they weren't. (By the way, Jesus' reference to Noah gives authority to the fact that the man lived, whether we want to accept the story of the ark and the flood or not. When we see something confirmed in the New Testament that happened in the Old, it tells us to take that story or situation seriously.)

I suspect that in Noah's day, people got used to the chaos because they lived life as if nothing would ever change. They married, had children, worked, celebrated . . . all of the things we would normally do unless we know disaster is coming. For instance, if we see a tornado barreling toward our house, we aren't likely to throw a party. We're going to take shelter. But in Noah's day, the people couldn't see the tornado, so they didn't heed the warnings.

That's how things will be before Jesus returns. The apostle Paul warns his readers, "While people are saying, 'There is peace and security,' then sudden destruction will come upon them . . . and they will not escape" (1 Thess. 5:3).

The people outside that ark did not escape the flood.

We need to remember that these Old Testament stories were given to us to teach us, to warn us, to instruct us. So whether you consider them fact or fiction, they speak truth, and they serve a purpose in God's economy. They send a message of what God intends for the future. He wants us to sit up and take notice.

Actually, He's been sending that message throughout time, first in the promise to Eve that He would provide a deliverer to crush the head of the serpent, the evil one. Then He offered the deliverance of the ark during the flood. He reaffirmed that message when He called Abraham to follow Him, and when

He sent the patriarchs and kings and prophets to tell of the coming one who would ultimately fulfill that first promise to Eve. He wants us to know Him, to repent and be safe, to be nestled in His place of refuge, His ark of safety. And He has given us many, many people along the way to tell us of His desire.

Sela is my fictional name for Shem's wife, and her story is also imagined. But stop for a moment and ask, *What if I stood in her place?* Noah had three sons, and they each took wives on that ark. They came from families who didn't join them.

Unlike Rahab of Joshua's day, Sela didn't get to save her family, even if she had tried. Rahab asked Joshua to let her family live, and Joshua told her that they would live if they entered her house and didn't leave. Noah's daughters-in-law could have asked their families to enter the ark because judgment was coming, but the Bible indicates that only eight people—Noah's family—did so.

We could argue that in Noah's day there was no army circling the city for people to fear. Those people had likely never seen any type of flood and couldn't imagine one, and they had no obvious reason to fear judgment. Rahab's people were no doubt living with violence, immorality, and corruption too, but they could see their enemy outside of the camp and had soldiers knocking on their door. And they were afraid.

Judgment is a scary prospect, isn't it? It's easier to avoid the thought of it than to face what might be true.

The people of Rahab's day feared. Maybe the people of Noah's day did too. But it didn't change their actions.

In the movie *The Fellowship of the Ring*, Aragorn meets up with Frodo and sees the ring he carries. He knows the truth, the history behind that ring. So he asks Frodo, "Are you frightened?"

Frodo responds, "Yes," to which Aragorn replies, "Not nearly frightened enough."

Of course, we are not hunted by Ringwraiths who want to harm us. Most of us don't have an army encircling our city. And even more of us don't live near a guy building a huge ship in the middle of a field with no water in sight.

But we still have reason for concern, even fear of judgment, if we do not know the promised deliverer who longs to keep us from a future such as the one the people of Noah's day endured. We have a loving Shepherd who wants to rescue us, searches for us. He gives us the picture of the Father who waits for the prodigal to return or the shepherd who searches the hills and fields for the pit where his lamb has fallen. He is the one who isn't satisfied with ninety-nine sheep. He wants all one hundred safely in His fold.

God our Shepherd wanted to rescue the people of Noah's day too, but they would not let Him. Noah preached truth anyway, and perhaps his family did the same. But all Noah could show the world was a boat—a boat being built on a piece of property likely far from water of any great size. What was there to fear in that? The chances of people thinking the guy was a little crazy are pretty high.

When we are living in our own world, doing what we want to do, it is really easy to scoff at anything that suggests we're wrong.

Noah withstood a lot of scoffing. And I would guess the women in his life did a lot of grieving. I know I would. I would be like Sela and run home to my parents and brothers and sisters and beg them to come with us. So what if

39

they stayed in the ark and the flood didn't come? They'd be laughed at when they came out, but at least they would be safe if what Noah said was true. Might she have reasoned that way? Does that seem too simple a faith through which someone could be truly saved?

It doesn't take huge faith to follow God. Sometimes all we have is faith the size of a small seed. But however small, it can be a first step.

God doesn't expect us to have the faith to move mountains when we first come to Him. That's what grace is for. He gives us time to get to know Him, just as He spent time with Adam and Eve in the garden. God has always, always wanted His creation to fellowship with, befriend, and know Him in a personal way. That is why chaos doesn't have to rule. God offers us so much more.

Imagine with Me

Birds twitter in the trees that survived the flood, and I am amazed at how quickly they have multiplied since the ark landed on the mountain. Noah and our sons considered dismantling the ark once the water had completely receded, but we had already sewn tents in which to live, and somehow none of us can bear to tear apart the home that kept us safe for well over a year.

How long ago it seems now. So much has changed since God promised to never flood the earth again. His colorful bow in the sky after every gentle rain always gives us hope. At first the rains caused fear and we would rush to the ark for safety. He wouldn't flood the earth again, would He—despite His promise? But eventually trust replaced fear.

God has been good to all of us. Our sons now have children, and I delight in our grandchildren, though I cannot deny that the wickedness in our hearts was not washed away with the water. If not for the sacrifices and God's grace to us, we could end up living in a world lost in chaos again.

Oh Lord, please keep us from destroying ourselves.

How often have I prayed thus? Each time I hold a new grandchild in my aging arms. Each time I hear my sons argue. And while Noah never seems to have a harsh word or thought, I cannot deny that I am sorely tempted to lash out or speak words I wish to take back. We are still a sinful people.

This truth hit me hardest the day our youngest son looked upon his father drunk and naked. Ham had no reason to enter Noah's tent, especially after they had all spent the night enjoying the fruit of the vine. But even after he walked into Noah's private quarters and discovered his father's state of undress, he should have simply turned his gaze away and covered his father with his robe. He should have shown respect.

Instead, he told his brothers, and as I listened to his mocking tone, dread filled my belly. It was dishonorable and wicked to speak of his father in such a way. But Ham—oh, my son! His heart has always been bent toward that hint of rebellion. And Noah, normally so gentle and righteous, cursed Ham's children and made them slaves to his brothers. Ham nearly picked up his family and moved away in his hurt and anger. But Keziah calmed his anger and begged that they stay. Ham agreed, but I look often on his children and wonder how long the fragile peace will last.

One day they will part ways with us. Now it is too dangerous to separate and try to live in the wilds with simply a wife and several young sons and daughters. But when they are grown . . .

I glance heavenward. The sky, bright and blue, feels thin, and the sun harsher since the canopy of water no longer protects us.

Will You keep us from destroying ourselves, Adonai Elohim?

It is a prayer that often lies unspoken on my lips. I thank Him after such prayers for preserving us, and when I see the rainbow, hope grows stronger. As He delivered us from the evil of the world that once was, He will deliver us again. He will send us a savior. I don't know how, but I know. Noah has spoken of it often, and I believe it every time I glance at the ark behind us on the mountain or see God's brilliance in the rainbow.

We cannot change the state of our hearts, but we do not have to fear that life will never improve. In time, perhaps even Ham's rebellious nature will mature and he will embrace Adonai as his brothers have. It is my constant prayer and hope.

From Chaos to Hope

She stood on the stage, a woman with a story and a need to share it. But she shared it cautiously, not proudly. Grateful. Relieved. Safe. Her world had been anything but safe.

While she had not been kidnapped by demigods of Noah's day, she had been the victim of human trafficking in our day. Right now. In our world. Our towns. And her traffickers could be my neighbors.[1]

1. Human trafficking is slavery, often sex slavery, and it is rampant and growing. Ministries like All Worthy of Love, Unshackled, and others offer refuge, and their volunteers roam the streets looking for victims in an attempt to show them love,

Unlike my imagined line between Seth's land and Cain's, we live in a world without borders against evil.

Historically, certain countries were known for being a refuge. In ancient Israel, where descendants of Shem lived, God provided cities of refuge. He told His people to care for the orphan, the widow, the foreigner, and the stranger, because they had been strangers in Egypt, which is Ham's land, ironically. City officials built walls for protection, but when the people and leaders were truly trusting in God, He was their protection.

We don't live in a world that trusts Him anymore. We live in a world not so different from that of Noah's day. Not a day goes by that the news does not show some violent act. Terrorism. Hatred. Riots. Tyranny. Greed. Corruption. Pride. As Noah's wife predicted and prayed against in my fictional account, we are destroying ourselves again.

The night I listened to the human trafficking victim speak, another woman also told her story. Hers was not of capture but of being threatened. Traffickers work in groups, she said, and when she saw the unmarked van and people approaching from different directions, she suspected enough to run and call the trafficking hotline.[2] She was one of those who got away. This woman escaped to hope again and to help those in need.

Noah finished that ark and boarded it with his wife and his sons and their wives and a whole lot of animals. They saw the evil approaching. Perhaps the mockers stood outside the

give them food and toiletries, and show them that there is hope. These victims become chained to their captors with invisible bonds. They are beaten down until they feel so worthless that they don't even try to escape.

2. The number for the National Human Trafficking Hotline is (888) 373-7888. Put it in your phone. It's worth keeping.

door and continued to hurl insults at them. I imagine those inside grieved a long time for those who would not listen to their message. Eventually, however, they came out of the ark and began to hope again.

Even amid the threat of coming judgment and the knowledge that our human hearts are flawed, there is hope. This is not the end, just as the flood was not the end. There is a new beginning of promise for those who believe in God.

Noah preached hope, but hope, like love, comes at a cost. It costs us our pride. Hope says, "Repent and be saved." Hope destroys chaos.

Peter, the apostle who was too bold for his own good when he thought Jesus was going to fix the chaos of his world, later said,

> Most importantly, I want to remind you that in the last days scoffers will come, mocking the truth and following their own desires. They will say, "What happened to the promise that Jesus is coming again? From before the times of our ancestors, everything has remained the same since the world was first created."
>
> They deliberately forget that God made the heavens long ago by the word of his command, and he brought the earth out from the water and surrounded it with water. Then he used the water to destroy the ancient world with a mighty flood. (2 Pet. 3:3–6 NLT)

God destroyed a world gone crazy, like the one Noah's wife knew. And if we are not careful—if we choose chaos over hope, sin over surrender, violence over peace, corruption over honesty, perversion over morality—we risk a similar wrath.

And yet . . . there is hope.

Because of Jesus, there is greater hope than Noah's wife had that day when she hoped with Sela that more people would join them. Or the day she hoped her son Ham would outgrow his rebellion. We already see great numbers of people coming to faith in Christ across the world. And more will come if we will believe, if we but ask God to bring them. I'm asking God for thousands of people to yet believe. Will you join me?

Ponder this

When we are struggling to survive in a world gone crazy, we need not fear the future. God promises to be with us.

The LORD himself goes before you and will be with you; he will never leave you nor forsake you. Do not be afraid; do not be discouraged. (Deut. 31:8 NIV)

When we trust Him with our struggles and our fears and our uncertain futures, we can rest on this promise.

Believe Him. Hope in Him. Count on Him. God can always be trusted because He never breaks His word.

Taking it further

1. When you look at the world around you today, do you feel hopeless, like things will never change? How can you turn hopelessness into hope?

2. Have you ever tried to convince someone to believe, only to be met with disdain? How has prayer for that person changed things?

3. Are you trusting God to be your "ark" of safety in a broken world? How did you come to know Him? How are you living like righteous Noah and sharing God's love and justice with people who seem lost in a crazy world? In what ways has God given you hope to share with those you love?

3

Sarai

Abandoned but Not Forgotten

(BASED ON GENESIS 12; 22)

If I Were Sarai

The Egyptian sun is wrapped in an orange-yellow glow as it kisses the edge of the Nile River. The view is different here on the roof of Pharaoh's palace. That I am allowed the privilege of this view surprised me, but guards stand near enough that I know I am not free to do anything but gaze on what used to be.

Abram, where are you?

Life was so different in Canaan. Different in Ur and Haran. Different before God spoke to Abram and told him to go. Go where? We weren't told to come to Egypt, and though

I blame myself, certain my actions to secure a child are the cause of my imprisonment, it is the feelings warring within me against Abram that trouble me most.

I have always trusted him. Even when we were children he had been my protector, not just my half brother. Though years separated us, we had a bond that grew into love—love that I thought would never leave me feeling lost, forsaken.

I swipe an unwanted tear, blaming the blaze of the setting sun. Ra, as they call it here, as though the flaming orb is a god to be worshiped. I know better.

Oh Adonai, where are You? Are You here? With me?

My stomach aches from avoiding food, and my heart aches with pain. How could Abram ask me to lie to protect him? What of me? He did nothing to rise up and speak. He did not admit the truth that I belong to him. Where is my protector now?

I walk away from the parapet and, flanked by guards before and behind, descend the stairs to the king's harem and the room set aside for me. The maid Hagar meets me to wash my feet, but I cannot muster a single word to say to her. She is foreign, her ways so strange.

This whole place is strange to me.

Oh God, I don't want to be here.

Is there a way to escape the guards? Can one be bribed? I glance at Hagar and wonder briefly if she can be trusted to help me. But the memory of the way I was escorted here drains my hope. Pharaoh's guards are everywhere, and unless Pharaoh sends me away, there is no escaping him. What will I do if he summons me as a man does his wife?

A shiver works through me. *Please, Adonai. Forgive my foolish actions of late and have mercy on me.*

I have no reason to believe Abram's God even hears my silent plea, but I believe in no other god, and there is no indication that Abram will be able to rouse his men to come to my aid. He has sold me to Pharaoh for the price of animals and servants. Is that all I am worth to him?

"Are you all right, mistress?" The servant Hagar speaks, though her voice barely registers in my ears.

I shake my head. "Why do you ask me this?" I cringe inwardly at how harsh I sound.

Hagar hesitates. "Forgive me, my lady, but there are tears on your cheeks. I fear perhaps you are offended by what you see here. I notice that you do not eat. Is there anything I can do?"

I brush away the tears and stare at this comely girl. So young and beautiful in her own Egyptian way. "I did not realize I showed such emotion. My thoughts are far from here. That is all."

I do not mean it as a dismissal, for I would enjoy someone's company, but after Hagar fits soft slippers onto my feet and bows low, she takes her leave.

A bone-weary ache fills me. What sense does it make for Pharaoh to think a woman of my age beautiful? I am long past seventy years!

I rise slowly, move to the bed, and curl onto my side, attempting sleep, when a knock stirs me. I ignore the intrusion, but a moment later, I hear footsteps come closer and feel someone kneel beside the bed.

"Mistress?" Hagar's voice.

I close my eyes, pretending to sleep.

"Mistress, I'm sorry to wake you. But I thought you should know tonight, before dawn brings the news unexpectedly."

I roll to a sitting position and meet Hagar's gaze. "What news?" My heart beats fast, fear rising.

"The king plans to call for you tomorrow. To meet you. You mustn't worry. These first meetings are just his way of taking your measure. He will not bring you to him at night for at least a month, perhaps even a year." Hagar looks at her hands.

My mind whirls, my thoughts a jumbled mess, but I manage to thank her and dismiss her again. Maybe this time she will stay away and keep her awful news with her.

Tomorrow. I will face Pharaoh alone with no one to help me? Abram will not be here, nor my servants. I cannot even be sure that Adonai will give me strength to stand up under this king's scrutiny. Just how far will this meeting go?

Fear heats my insides like sudden flame. I cannot go. And yet I have to go. I am completely alone, and I have no choice.

In Our World

Duplicity. Denial. In a word, lies. As Abram asked of Sarai. The very thought of being asked to lie to protect someone else at your expense . . . could you do it? This isn't the only time we hear of people lying to save either their own skin or someone else's. Later in Scripture David lies to protect himself from the Philistines.

So was Abram wrong to ask Sarai to lie for him and say she was his sister? Technically, she *was* his half sister, so was it really a lie?

We could debate the question for years to come, but the truth is, the Bible does not condone lying. In fact, Solomon lists it as one of the seven things the Lord hates. Yet there is no mention of condemnation of Abram or David or Isaac when they used these tactics to save their lives. We could say the culture allowed such things, but I doubt we can use that excuse. God has always been pretty clear about the subject. Wasn't it the lying serpent that got us into all this trouble in the first place?

Despite how lying entered the world, we all face this vice, don't we? But when you are lied to or lied about, how does that make you feel? Have you ever had a lie get you into trouble when you were the innocent party? Has a misunderstanding ever led to someone lying and you getting hurt?

Now, Sarai agreed to lie for Abram, so they were both in on the deceit. But only one of them ended up paying for the lie. Doesn't seem quite fair, does it?

Sarai lied to protect her husband from being killed by an ancient Pharaoh whose name we don't know. Realistically, they both should have trusted God for that protection because they knew He had made covenant promises to them. Instead, they sought a human solution.

Do you ever do that? I know I do. And even faithful Abram had his weaknesses, as we all do.

I'm a pretty trusting person, so it always takes me by surprise when I discover someone has lied to me. After the initial shock wears off, I'm not quite sure what to do next. Their lies might not land me in Pharaoh's palace, but I definitely will be more careful of what I say to them next time. Trust, once lost, is not easily regained. Maybe it was different in Abram's culture because Sarai went along with this type of lie more than once—perhaps often in their travels through foreign lands.

But what do we do when someone's choice puts us in a compromising situation? That happened to me many years ago when I was rather new to the working world. I had a job in a prestigious company that I thought was going to be a great fit for me. But as time went on, my superiors started making "suggestions" that I rephrase the way I answered the phone: "Tell them the boss isn't in. It's not good business to say that he's not available."

Except the boss *was* in. He just didn't want to talk to whoever was on the other end of the line. Trouble was, as a Christian with a strong sense of right and wrong, I didn't believe saying such a thing was right. It was a lie to say he wasn't in when I could see him through the glass. But business has its ways of doing things, and the bosses wanted to give the impression that they missed the call because they were out doing something else. That impression seemed more palatable to them.

This reminds me of another time when I gave birth to one of our sons. I won't give you the gory details, but I will say that I was in a lot of pain afterward because of some medication the hospital staff was giving me, which added to the pain of a cesarean section. They claimed they were trying but unable to reach my doctor. My doctor later claimed, "If I'd only known . . ."

So who was telling the truth? I'll never know for sure, but one of them was not being fully honest, and I paid for their dishonesty.

I suppose on a really small scale I understand how Sarai might have felt. But given our different cultures and what she was up against, probably not. While a doctor might have seemed like Pharaoh (an all-powerful bully), he wasn't. And I at least had help in seeking relief from suffering. Sarai faced her situation alone.

But lies of any kind hurt us, don't they? Especially when they are aimed at people we love.

This memory is of long ago and, thankfully, no longer causes emotional pain. When the two letters arrived in the mail, I was shocked at the words. The second letter I couldn't even read. I handed it to my husband, and it took me many months before I gave myself permission to read it—once I'd gotten past the hurt of the first one.

The letters carried a personal attack on the character of my family, all because we had chosen to resign certain ministry positions. But the words were not true. They were written in anger and seemed to want to intimidate us, but they did not speak truth. Whether verbal or written, these kinds of things sting.

This sort of slander is far-reaching. The ripple effect goes far beyond our personal hurt. I wonder if the one causing the hurt ever stops to realize how much their actions will trickle down through the years, cross family lines, and spread through friendships and churches and communities. When they choose to break that trust, say those words, or think only of themselves, does the damage they've caused ever occur to them?

Whether we've known them or not, we all have a myriad of ancestors. When I was born, I had two grandfathers. By my third birthday, one of them had died. My other grandfather had moved across the country. I'm told that he was a rather angry man, although I didn't know him well. This was not the age of the computer or webcam when we might have talked with my grandparents frequently. Even a phone call in those days was costly. I think I can count on one hand the number of times I saw my grandfather in person throughout my life. I wish that could have been different.

When you grow up with half of your family on the other side of the country, you feel like you are missing a part of yourself. So the curious part of me asked questions. When we did visit, I would sit with my aunt and ask her about my cousins and aunts and uncles and grandparents, who all lived in the same state.

It wasn't until much later that I found pictures and genealogical records that gave me a glimpse into my grandfather's world. In truth, the records tell two different tales. In one, it seems as though he could have been adopted at a younger age, though when asked who his parents were, he named his birth parents, so it was likely he knew them. In another place the record showed that his mother died when he was in his teens, but his father still lived. If this second scenario was true, you would think my great-grandfather would have kept his son close. He'd lost his wife. And his son, though a teen, was old enough to work by then, to help him out. Because the records are sketchy, I cannot know which version is true or the reasons why. I can only know that another couple adopted my grandpa probably sometime after his mom's death. I don't know if he ever saw his birth father again.

Perhaps that's why Grandpa couldn't control his anger. And why my dad grew up believing that anger out of control is a bad thing—something he couldn't let rule his own behavior.

We all have reasons for the things we do. Abram is called a man of faith, God's friend, and so he was. But he was also tempted to fear for his safety. He could believe God would give him a son one day, but he didn't quite trust God to keep him alive to have that child when he entered a foreign land. I can relate to that waffling fear! Can you?

It is a simple thing, especially when we are young, to believe in Jesus, to trust God with our eternal salvation. Yet to trust God with our daily lives—especially during those times of feeling alone—is so much harder, isn't it?

What kind of hurt or emotional pain are you facing right now? Does it still stick like a knife in your gut? Or has it slipped away with the grace of forgiveness?

If I told you that I have never been lied to since those long-ago times, I'd be lying, because we go through life dealing with people. And people are messy. *I'm* messy (and not just my closets)!

I wish I could tell you that my grandpa died a loving, peaceful man. How I would have loved to have a closer relationship with him. But my dad was not close to him because of that anger wall, which held more than bad memories. The anger never really went away despite my grandpa's Christian beliefs.

Yes, Christians are messy too because the truth is, we're all broken people with pasts we can't erase and sometimes can't forgive. When we choose not to forgive, however, we set ourselves up for a life of bitterness and merciless judgment of others. We lose all ability to live the grace we were given when we first believed.

I would like to believe that Abram and Sarai had a great marriage after that incident in Egypt. All indications point that way at first, but Genesis is a book of dysfunctional families, and Abram's was no better than the rest. Sarai didn't learn during her experience that she wasn't in control. She still couldn't quite accept that God *could* give her a child—especially after she hit menopause. Can I get an agreement here? I'm old enough to tell you that if I were suddenly pregnant, it would be *all* God because I'm way past the point of having children or wanting to start all over again! (Now, grandchildren—that's a different story!)

After Egypt, Abram and Sarai faced years of ups and downs in their marriage. I'm sure they had tender moments as well as grievous ones. But I don't know if their marriage was ever truly healed after Abraham went to offer Isaac on God's altar. I know how I would have felt if it were me, and the Bible indicates that Sarah and Abraham didn't live in the same area after that incident. Maybe I'm wrong, but that's what my study shows.

Those lies I've faced? I'm over most of them, but I still face others. As long as life lasts I will, but I'm not sure the shock of discovering what is actually true will ever get easier.

My grandpa? He's been gone a long time. I pray in the end that he was finally rid of the hurt and pain he carried. My dad took us to visit his family one year and shared Jesus with the family members who lived there. His dad didn't give him the assurance of salvation that his mom did, but that doesn't mean doubt kept him from knowing the truth deep down. I've learned that only God has the right to judge another person's heart. He's the only one who sees what's going on behind the scenes.

As for Abram and Sarai, I can imagine Sarai dreaded those moments when they were forced to move into hostile territory and she was asked yet again to lie to protect the one who was shirking his duty to protect her. Maybe Abram had a twisted sense that by keeping himself alive he *was* protecting her, but it's hard to believe he could have done anything to get her out of the king's palace, short of telling the truth.

A lot of rejection and denial can be avoided with truth.

Imagine with Me

I awaken early that morning in a cold sweat, my body drenched. Was it a dream? I look to the place Abraham has been to find that he has already arisen. Dawn has yet to crest the eastern sky, and he is no longer a young man who hurries to his work each day. Where could he have gone?

I notice the lamp still resting in the niche in the ground, away from the edges of the tent. I push up from the earth and force my aged body to pick it up and follow its light from the tent to the compound. There, near the fire pit, Abraham stands with Isaac and two servants. They carry wood and fire as if they are about to offer a sacrifice. Whatever for?

I move to join them. "Were you going to leave without telling me?"

Abraham looks at me as though he barely sees me. At last his gaze focuses on mine. "The Lord has sent me to offer a sacrifice. We will be gone about a week."

I stare at him, then at my son. "Just the two of you?" I know the servants are only with them for protection. "And why so far?" The request made no sense, but I know Abraham well enough to know that he is not lying. He has heard God's voice again, a voice even I know too well. One does not disobey such a voice when you know to whom it belongs. I have also seen Him in human form, and He causes both fear and awe to live inside my heart.

"He has His reasons." My husband says no more, and I know I will not be able to pull words from him. He turns to Isaac and motions to the servants to start for the road. He looks back at me and kisses my cheek. "Do not fear." But at the very expression on his face and those three words, fear suddenly causes my heart to beat too fast.

Isaac kisses me as well and holds me tightly for a brief moment. He does not seem to fear, but I can sense questions in his eyes.

"Be safe," I say weakly as the only men I love walk away. I watch them until I can no longer see them, then move to the fire pit and sink onto a rock lest my legs give way.

My maid joins me. "I will bring you food and drink."

She hurries off before I can tell her that I am not hungry. Why was Abraham so reticent to tell me what God had said? Why could he not offer a sacrifice here as he has always done? Why was I not invited to join him?

Merciless questions beat against me during those torturous days of waiting. He has left me alone yet again to face uncertainty I cannot understand. I search my mind for reasons, but they elude me. Then all at once on the third day, I look up from my spinning and call to my maid.

"Did you see an animal—a ram or lamb or goat—with the servants who accompanied your master? It was dark and I did not look for it." Surely Abraham had taken more than wood and fire.

She looks at me as though her mind is reliving that morning, trying to recall each detail. At last she shakes her head. "I did not see an animal, mistress. Perhaps they gathered it from the flocks on their way."

I nod. Of course. It had been so early, they would not have had time to search the flocks for the perfect sacrifice. Abraham would have gone first to the flocks, then continued on to the place God had told him to go.

The thought leaves me less restless as I move between working and pacing my tent. At moments when I feel my emotions will snap, I bark at my servants and walk to the edge of the field, straining for some sign of their return.

A week, he had said. I count the days and am the first one waiting near the road they will take home. But when I see my son, my only son, his appearance carries something I cannot understand. He is different somehow, and it hurts me to see it. Am I simply despairing that he now seems more of a man?

I fall into his arms and weep. He clings to me and pats my back, but he does not speak.

In fact, weeks pass before Isaac speaks of their trip to me. Abraham has given me few details, but it is Isaac who finally explains what had happened, that there had been no lamb other than him, and how God had spared him.

"Your own father would have killed you." I do not shout or raise my voice as I speak, for I can barely lift my words above a whisper.

"God had asked him to, but God also stopped him. It was a test, Ima. A test for us both." Isaac's words are meant to soothe, I know that. But they do not soothe. They only heat the anger that had begun the day Abraham left with but a few words to me.

I do not tell him immediately. I cannot make a decision so quickly, but in time, I will convince Isaac to move my tent to another place, away from Beersheba to Hebron. Away from my husband. Though I know Abraham loves Isaac and me, this . . . this is too much. I cannot abide it. And the more I am forced to deal with Abraham, the worse I feel. I have no choice. I need time away. Space to accept . . .

Can I *ever* accept this? I am not sure.

From Duplicity to Trust

Solomon mentions lying in Proverbs 6:16–19 with these words:

> There are six things the Lord hates—
>   no, seven things he detests:
> haughty eyes,
>   a lying tongue,
>   hands that kill the innocent,
> a heart that plots evil,
>   feet that race to do wrong,
> a false witness who pours out lies,
>   a person who sows discord in a family. (NLT)

It's interesting that lying is listed twice in these verses—a lying tongue and a false witness. Both are liars. Both cause a world of harm.

If only we could speak truth from honest hearts. But I suspect there are many reasons we seal the truth in tight lips and closed hearts. We don't even want to discuss why. In reality, we live in a world of denial.

Could it be that we are ashamed of the truth? Afraid that if other people really know us, they will turn away? Think ill of us? Condemn us? But the only people who would do that are people who do not love us in the first place. Friends will leave. Family is not always trustworthy. But there is one who sticks closer than a brother. God can always be trusted with the things we hide. And once we are honest with Him and with ourselves, we can begin to be honest with the people in our lives who truly love us for who we are, despite anything we've ever done.

I hope you have people like that in your life. I know I do. I also have people I would love as long as life lasts, no matter what—and I'm simply human. Think how much more God cares for us!

I wonder if things would have been different if Sarai had explained to Abram that she didn't want to lie. What if she'd appealed to his trust in God to help him to seek a better way? Scripture does not tell us the things they might have discussed beyond this point, so we can only speculate.

And then there is that issue of God asking Abraham to shed the blood of his son on an altar. This is something God calls murder (Lev. 20:1–3), and we know from Scripture that this was a test of Abraham's faith (Gen. 22:1). God had no intention of allowing Abraham to go through with the deed. And Abraham believed God enough to trust Him to raise Isaac to life again (Heb. 11:17–19).

But Sarah was not privy to the words God spoke or the thoughts running through Abraham's mind. She may have trusted him, but we can also imagine why this could have caused her deep pain.

When she was in Pharaoh's court, God intervened so the truth would come out and Sarai would be restored to Abram as his wife. In the case of Abraham and Isaac and the altar, God was also the one who intervened, but not in the way anyone had expected.

God may not come to our aid quite so visibly, but we can know that He is there if we seek Him. That's a promise in Scripture we can count on (Jer. 29:13; Matt. 7:7–8).

Sarai is later commended as a woman of faith (Heb. 11:11), but in that moment in Pharaoh's palace, I suspect her faith wavered. Doubts often assail us when we are faced with the fiery storms of life. But years later when God spoke truth directly to her, not just through her husband, I think His promise changed her. Up until then, she probably believed, but she'd also been controlling, strong-willed, and one who liked to fix things.

Aren't we often the same? We are hurt, sometimes torturously so, and we struggle to make our world right again.

Sometimes trials reveal the truth we deny to our own hearts. Maybe when Sarai finally found that truth—when God caught her lies and turned them around—she saw that He could be trusted. She wasn't alone in her pain. She wasn't cursed or forgotten in her struggles. God blessed her in spite of them.

But let's face it, Sarai was human. Though the Bible does not tell us there was a rift between Abraham and Sarah after the altar ordeal, it does say that Abraham lived in Beersheba and Sarah died in Hebron. Now, maybe by then they had both moved to Hebron. But several versions of Scripture say that Abraham went to mourn for her. One says he "went in" to mourn for her (Gen. 23:2). So did he go to Hebron from wherever he was to mourn when he heard of her death? Or was he living there with her and he went into her tent to mourn? Again, there appears to be reason for speculation, but it is interesting that the next major event in Scripture is her death. While we do not know how many years passed after the sacrifice, we see nothing more happen between Abraham and Sarah.

Even though Sarai may have failed or felt her faith waver later in life, God did not abandon her. We are never promised a life of constant ease. More often the opposite is true. We live a life of struggle on this earth, in these bodies. And though we might see a miracle in one instance, that doesn't mean we won't face future hardships.

When life hits hard and we're forced to face fire alone— when those closest to us betray us, reject us, or leave us; when people we love break our trust; when life isn't going the way we had planned—we can seek the truth or live the lie. We can let God speak to our hearts or shut our ears and refuse to listen.

Sarai started out choosing the lie, as her husband asked her to do. Eventually, though, they both came face-to-face with Truth, and soon after, their long-awaited promised blessing—the one they had started on a long journey to receive—came. And his coming changed everything.

Ponder this

When we feel forsaken or alone or like the world is against us, remember God's words to Israel:

> *I will not forget you.*
> *Behold, I have engraved you on the palms of my hands.*
>   *(Isa. 49:15–16)*

While His words may have been to the people of Zion, we can apply them to all who believe because of what Jesus has done for us. Remember. Trust. We are *not* forgotten. Ever. Our names are etched on Jesus' nail-scarred hands.

Taking it further

1. Have you ever been betrayed or lied to by someone you love? How did you feel?
2. Has someone you trusted ever asked you to do something you know is wrong? Did you discuss it with

them and find a better way, or did you go along with their bad advice? What was the outcome of your choice? How would you do things in the future if you are faced with such a choice again?

3. When facing life's trials, how do you feel? If your feelings are negative, how do you handle them? If they are positive, how does that change your perspective? Do you believe that God will never leave you, even if everyone else does? Why or why not?

4

Hagar

Does Anybody See Me?

(BASED ON GENESIS 16; 21)

If I Were Hagar

The pallet beneath me cradles my aching back, and I draw in a breath, relieved. It was foolish to run. I understand that now, and yet . . . had God really met me there?

The God Who Sees Me. I had named Him that day beside the spring. He promised this child would be a man with many descendants. I will not be left without comfort. If only I felt some of that comfort now.

A sigh escapes as darkness shrouds me. Abram has assured me that I will suffer no more abuse from Sarai, but that does not stop the words *He* had spoken from burning in my mind.

Return to your mistress and submit to her authority. I am still a slave, sold to a couple who should be grateful to me.

I want to go home. My heart yearns with that longing. But I have no home. I had played the fool in Egypt, and my father had thought me a servant to give away. Here I am neither respected nor pampered, merely treated as any other person belonging to Abram and Sarai.

I wish I had never heard their names.

A prick in my spirit gives me pause. I rest my hands on the sides of my belly, longing again for the feel of the baby's kick. It is wrong to disrespect Abram, for his God has spoken to him and to me. The thought causes a shiver to sweep over me. A healthy fear accompanies the feeling, and I rise slowly and creep from my tent to gaze at the night sky. Stars so brilliant they take my breath away spread from one side of the earth's canopy to the other. Is that where God lives?

Do You see me now? Do You always see me? Will You come to me again?

"Hagar."

I jump at Abram's voice behind me. "My lord," I say, turning to face him. I bow, for in that moment, I do not know what else to do. Why is he here near my tent?

"You should be resting," he says, his voice gentle. Is that a hint of fear in his tone?

"I know." I straighten. "And I will. It's just . . . He spoke to me and sent me back, and I cannot help but wonder where He lives. This God of yours. Does He reside among the stars?" My people worship the sun and revere the heavenly bodies, but not one of the gods of my people had spoken to me in the form of a man.

"Our God is a spirit, though He can appear to us as a man or call to us from the heavens. Where He lives, who can tell?" The lines along Abram's aged face are visible in the moonlight. How strange it seems that this man is my husband and yet not my husband. Worse yet, I will never know the love of a man my equal or my age.

Oh God of Abram, my heart cries even as I hold Abram's gaze. Will loving the child be enough? What will happen to me when Sarai claims my son as her own? I will be his nurse, nothing more.

"Hagar?"

I shake myself, realizing that my thoughts have drifted. "Yes, my lord."

"You will not run again. Will you?" He *is* afraid. I have not mistaken the fear in his tone. "I am sorry for the way you were treated."

I stare. The head of this tribe of men and women is apologizing to me?

He just wants his son, not you.

I fight the argument rising within me. Even if my thoughts are true, I have to stay. His God has made that clear enough.

"I will not run again," I say, clasping my suddenly clammy hands together. I study them, for I cannot face him again. At least he has noticed my existence. Running has benefited me that much.

"Thank you." He tips my chin to look into my eyes. "Our God will bless you for your kindness."

My eyes grow wide. I cannot stop the disbelief that Abram would say such a thing to me now, after he had given Sarai permission to treat me as the servant I am. When he is in the fields, what is there to stop her from taking out her anger on me again?

My heart pounds as he lets his hand drop to his side. He clears his throat. "Rest well, Hagar." He moves on from me then.

I turn to watch him walk to his tent. His shoulders seem to droop more than they had before I left the camp.

He cares about the child, not you.

The thoughts plague me as I glance at Sarai's tent, now cloaked in darkness, then duck beneath the curtains of my own. Did God stop me on the road because He cares for me or because He wants to preserve Abram's seed?

I crawl onto the pallet once more and stare at the lone clay lamp nearby. Its dancing flicker reminds me somehow of Egypt, of our ritual dances at the festivals to our gods. My son should know about my heritage, shouldn't he? Or will Sarai forbid him from knowing anything of Egypt? It is obvious the woman detests my homeland even more than she seems to detest me now.

I close my eyes against a sudden headache. *O God Who Sees Me, help me. I came back to do as You asked, but I do not know if I can live this way. I want someone to accept me for who I am . . . to love me.*

Has anyone ever loved me?

But gods do not love. They expect obedience. They demand sacrifice. They require worship. They do not love. Even if Abram's God sees me, I have no certainty that He wants me. Perhaps I am simply needed in this moment. If only I could see Him again, then I would ask Him. *If You see me, do You also care for me?*

The night wanes and I try to sleep, but the questions keep me awake, haunting me.

In Our World

Have you ever longed to feel loved? Wondered if anyone accepted you? Wanted to belong *somewhere*?

Those thoughts came to me often in my childhood. The quiet introvert, I wasn't good at sports, only academics. Added to that, I was not thin like the pretty girls. By today's standards, I don't know why weight became such an issue for me. When I look back at pictures, I see I wasn't as overweight as I thought. But thin mattered, especially if you weren't athletic. I was neither.

So I walked to and from school mostly alone. I pretended to be Marcia Brady as I swung on the swing set during recess, and I studiously did my work. To say I had a good self-image would be a lie. I didn't like myself or dislike myself. I just preferred to escape into fiction or fantasy. I knew my parents loved me, but I didn't feel liked by many of my peers.

Have you been there? How many lonely little girls and boys sit unnoticed in classrooms today? My husband volunteers at a junior high school nearby, and there are some like I was—quiet, "good" kids. And then there are those who constantly cause trouble. I wonder if at a heart level they are really that much different from each other. One seems to want to hide, unnoticed. The other is begging for attention. But both of them want to be accepted.

All of us are looking for someone to appreciate us, to *see* us, to love us, yes?

That girl on the playground with the Marcia Brady complex got a little older, and one day as she sat in her sixth grade class, her teacher, Mr. Murrell, announced that his wife was going to have a baby. He said that if it was a girl, they were going to name her after one of the girls in the class. We all looked at each other, wondering who that girl would be. He was a favorite teacher in the school, and any girl would have been honored. Of course, I knew that the baby would probably be named Antoinette. Antoinette had such a beautiful, roll-off-your-tongue, unique name.

Not long after that announcement, Mr. Murrell stood in front of the class and told us that his wife did give birth to a baby girl. I doodled on my notebook and half listened until I heard my name. *Jill*. Jill? I looked around. Since I was the only Jill in that elementary school at the time, I couldn't point to anyone else.

Me? He picked my name? I didn't even like my name! But maybe that was more because I didn't like myself all that much.

I wonder if Hagar liked who she was. The Bible doesn't tell us much about her, though there are suggestions that she came from Egyptian royalty, which is why I depicted her that way in my novel *Sarai*.

Regardless of her background, we do know that she was Sarai's servant and she bore Abram a son. We also know that she is the only woman who named God! Actually, she was the only *person* who named God. Every other time, God revealed His name to those He visited. To Abram He was *Adonai El Elyon*, Lord God Most High. To Moses, *I Am*. He wouldn't tell Jacob His name but instead named Jacob *Israel*. But Hagar named Him *The God Who Sees Me*.

As Mr. Murrell named his daughter after me—though I admit, the comparison may seem flimsy—so Hagar named God in a way that honored Him, the way *she* saw Him. As my teacher took notice of a lonely, introverted, overweight girl and liked her name, so God took notice of a frightened slave and cared for her. I can't help but think that Hagar was changed when she realized the God of Abram saw her, called her by name, gave her instructions, and made her a promise.

While Hagar returned and might have still struggled with the people around her, as I have often struggled to feel accepted throughout my life, she couldn't forget that there was one who knew. Who saw her. And He knew her name.

Imagine with Me

The sun glares harsh in the wilderness, the land barren and often filled with only desert brush and sand. Endless sand. If not for the caves and the occasional tree, I think I would go mad for lack of color, though I have learned that even in the wilderness there is beauty and flowers spring up in odd places. I am still able to create beautiful dyes to clothe my son in the colors of a chieftain, for that is what he is. I glance up at the sound of his footfalls and watch from a distance as he kisses his wife, the wife I found for him in Egypt.

My life is fuller than I imagined it could ever be that long-ago day when Abraham sent us away from his camp with a water skin and little else. The memory lingers a moment as I stand in the arch of the cave I have made my home. Sarah was the one to blame, as usual. If not for her son, Isaac, my Ishmael would have inherited his father's wealth.

Instead, she caught Ishmael laughing at her son and forced Abraham to send us away. I still question why he did not send us with provisions. It has been a burr in my side for decades, but most days I forget. There is no use dwelling on what should have been.

What if God had not met me in the desert? I've thought long on that as well. The skin of water soon ran out, and I was certain Abraham had sent us to our deaths. I could not bear to watch my son die of thirst, but we were in the wastelands and there were no wells in sight. So I set him down under one of the low-hanging bushes to shade him and walked away so I could not hear his pitiful cries.

A tear slips down my cheek at the memory. Even now the pain brings tears. How had my life come to this? If only I had stayed in Egypt, been content with what was there, I could be living in the palace or in a home as mistress with servants of my own. I could dip my toes in the lotus pools and gaze upon the grand obelisks and carvings of my people.

But I wonder sometimes if Abraham's God allowed this path on which I have found myself. I cannot say I am completely angry, for without Abraham, I would not have my son, and he is worth ten thousand men.

The cost to Ishmael, though, is great. He grew up without his father's guiding hand. He learned to survive in the wilderness with his mother's help and none other those many years, until men began to join him and he formed a mighty band.

All because the God Who Sees Me saw once more. I did not face the awful pain of watching my son die, for God called to me there and showed me a well of water my eyes had not seen. He told me not to fear and promised to make Ishmael a great nation, and by the number of sons his wife has already borne, I believe Him!

Sometimes I wonder why I so easily doubt. Twice now Abraham's God has spoken to a lowly Egyptian, a foreigner, a slave in the eyes of most—but apparently valuable to God. My heart stirs with the thought, gratitude filling me. I used to think I would never know love, but now a family who pours love over me surrounds me. I am no longer one whom nobody sees. God has seen me and made my life one of wealth and beauty. What more could I ask for than that?

From Invisible to Noticed

Hagar's story hit home to me more recently and with far more certainty than that memory of a kind teacher. I had faced some serious struggles with empty-nest syndrome after homeschooling for twelve years. I also faced some major personal trials that I had not expected, and the truth was, I felt like I was drowning in emotional pain.

I once asked my Facebook followers which is worse: physical pain or emotional pain. Hands down, emotional pain topped the list. You can hear what I'm saying, can't you? Maybe you've been there too. When the darkness closes in so deep it scares you—because sometimes life feels like the shadow of death—you know the feeling. If you can relate, you are not alone.

Job faced it when he wished he had never been born. Elijah faced it when he feared for his life and simply couldn't go on. Jonah faced it when he grew angry with God for doing exactly what he didn't want God to do—spare his enemies. Paul felt it at some point because he declared that "we despaired of life" (2 Cor. 1:8).

David faced it too. In the 23rd Psalm, the most famous of them all, he wrote of the valley of the shadow of death. Some say this was in reference to a dangerous valley he'd passed through with the sheep. His reflection on those moments tells us that he only got through the valley because God was with him. I would say every person in Scripture who faced emotional pain and despaired even of life got through it only by the grace of God. It's how we all survive the dark places of life.

Have you been in that dark place where you wondered, *Does God even see me? Is He listening? Does He really love me?* Have you been in that place where you cried out, because without His grace you wondered if you were going to make it?

I understand. I've been there too. During one of those times when God didn't seem to be hearing my prayers, I could feel myself falling into that shadow of darkness. I had prayed and fasted and prayed with my husband and prayed night and day, and still the answer was, *Wait. Don't give up. Wait.*

Wait really ought to be a four-letter word—if you know what I mean.

But what else could I do? Still, waiting did not erase the pain that had settled deep in my heart. Emotional pain can be like grief that never ends. It might take a breather for a while, but when you remember the circumstance, the pain returns, and you're clinging to a life raft all over again.

That's how I felt when I went to a conference a few years ago. It was a speakers' conference, and I honestly was not sure why I was going. Every door had opened to get me in, but it was a lot of money and I didn't know if speaking was what God had for me. I mean, really? I write fiction most of the time. Who wants to listen to a storyteller talk about life?

But I went—rather, I backed into the process—and decided just to learn. I had no agenda. I hardly knew a single person except a few of those on staff, but I dragged my husband along for moral support (and so he could have some fun golfing and visiting a racetrack—hobbies we don't share in common), and I sat in classes and listened.

Can I tell you a story of what God did at that conference? He showed up. And *He saw me!* Everywhere I turned, I met incredible women who for one reason or another felt called by God to speak a word over me or pray for me, encourage me, and uplift me. I felt almost guilty—and even said so—that they should pray for me when we all have struggles. Women there were facing far worse things than I was.

But He saw!

One dear young woman sat next to me during one of the classes. The speaker was telling a story—and trust me, when this woman speaks, people listen! She made me laugh and cry. But the crying came far easier when she came to her final story, and the young woman next to me noticed. (When you're fishing for a Kleenex and swiping at tears, it's rather hard *not* to notice!) She told me later that she could feel my emotional pain. She saw more than my tears. She took my hand and afterward told me that she felt God wanted her to tell me something, which ended up being a great encouragement to me.

If that had been an isolated incident, I might have blown it off. I guess you could say I'm not as easily wowed as Hagar, but then I didn't meet God in the flesh. Yet I did meet Him at that conference. And then I knew why a woman who might never be a speaker was sent there. It was for Him to heal my heart. He sent me to North Carolina for some soul healing. Apparently He couldn't do the same work in me in Michigan. Maybe I wouldn't let Him.

I can't say that I came home completely healed of emotional struggles. That *wait* word? I'm still there in some of life's circumstances, and I believe I always will be, because the moment God ends one waiting period, there will be another. It's part of life. It's not something we like but something we cannot avoid.

We are all going to face times in our lives when we feel overlooked or even ignored, and that's going to hurt if we let it. We can run away like Hagar did and hold our hurts close to our hearts. We can avoid relationships that might wound us. Or we can go back, believe what God says about us—He *sees* us—wait on Him to do the work only He can do, and forgive the things that are ours to forgive.

Scripture and history tell us that Hagar's life in Abraham's camp didn't last long. Less than twenty years later, she was walking away again, this time with her son into a future she couldn't fathom. I can imagine how all of the memories of that first trip toward Egypt came rushing back, only this time she feared for the life of her son.

And God met her again. Hagar. A woman. An outcast. Not one among the lineage of the people God had chosen. But one among the lineage of people God wanted to save. God saw her. And He considered her life precious to Him.

He sees us too, my friend. Unlike any other god the world has known, He loves us. We are precious in His eyes. And no amount of hurt in the world can ever take that knowledge from us.

Ponder this

When we walk through this journey called life, we are going to face things that cause hurt and pain. And we may feel unloved and unaccepted. Perhaps we may not even like ourselves all that much. But God says,

Fear not, for I have redeemed you;
I have called you by name, you are mine.
(Isa. 43:1, emphasis mine)

God accepts us. He *sees* us. He calls each one of us personally—by our name. When we come to Him, He wraps us in His everlasting love. And when He declares, "You are mine," we know that nothing can ever separate us from His love.

Taking it further

1. Have you ever felt invisible, like no one sees the real you? How did you handle those feelings? Did you push past them or revert inward?

2. Has there ever been a time in your life when you know that God saw you, and He did something or sent someone to show you how much He cares? How did you feel in that moment? How did it change your outlook on your situation and on God? Can you give an example of how you have been able to pass on that same gift to someone else?

3. Are you in a vulnerable place right now that makes you want to run away from your struggles? What kind of solution might involve staying and working it out? If you are not in a safe place, how might you go about seeking help? If you are in a dark place, please don't carry the burden alone. God sees. Seek help from people, yes. But don't forget to ask Him to help you too.

5

Melah
(Lot's Wife)

Don't Look Back
(BASED ON GENESIS 19)

If I Were Lot's Wife

Noise filters through the open window, the rowdy boys returning from the fields, no doubt heading for the gaming houses where they can drink wine until they are besotted. I rub my aching temples and glance toward the hall that leads to the front door, for Lot surely will come soon. The girls have long since returned from the homes of their betrothed, and servants have begun chopping vegetables for stew.

I should get up. Do something. But a sense of unrest has troubled me for many months. I wish I understood the reason. Sometimes I feel a strange listlessness and I know I grieve my son's loss. Sometimes I am anxious over the details of Kammani's upcoming wedding. Joy often eludes me.

I wonder if I've ever known joy. Sarai seemed to have captured the elusive feeling at times. Abram surely seemed to, especially after he had heard from his God.

But Lot is not an easy man to live with, and though I know I can usually get him to give in to my way of thinking, sometimes I wish I had never married him. Never *had* to marry him.

If I had never trusted him, had seen past his charm and flattering ways and kept myself from him until after the marriage, or had married someone else, things would have been different. I wouldn't be living in this foreign land, for I would not have been bound to him and had to follow him as he followed Abram. If I'd known he would make such a foolish choice as to leave our families, I would never have agreed. If only we had never left Ur. Or Haran. If only we could go back.

A sigh escapes as I rise from the plush bed I insisted Lot purchase. I clutch my wine chalice and slowly make my way to the heated space where a fire pit sits near the center and a pot hangs above a low fire. The servants have been forced to cook the food indoors rather than in the courtyard as most of the townswomen are used to doing, for fear of the violent crowds that roam the streets at all hours of the day. The arrangement is not ideal even with the open windows.

I glance at the window now. The rowdy men have quickly moved on, and semi-quiet has descended on our neighborhood. Lot must be taking his time at the city gate, for normally he is home before the men come in from the fields.

I stumble, for I have already consumed too much wine, and cling tight to the chalice lest it spill. I move forward and brace myself against the entryway. My head spins slightly. I should have taken cheese and bread with the wine, but I was too weary to rise to get them.

I blink at the mess the servants have made of the vegetables and see that the water in the pot over the low fire has not even begun to boil. "Dinner will be late at the rate you are moving." I try to be stern, but my head pounds too much.

The sound of male voices draws our attention away from the work. The front door opens. The voices grow louder. I set the chalice on a board where a servant works and hurry back to my room. Has Lot brought visitors? I glance in the bronze mirror to examine my wan skin and dull eyes. I will never hold Sarai's beauty. The thought grates.

"Abba has brought strange men to the house!" Kammani comes from the sitting area, and Ku-aya hurries to join her in my room.

I move out of the room again, careful to keep from staggering. I close my eyes briefly to clear my head as Kammani and Ku-aya follow me.

"Bake bread without yeast and bring out our finest cheeses and wine." Lot speaks to one of the servants, and his tone holds a hint of urgency. Whatever for? A few simple men?

"Melah, there you are," he says, noticing me. "I invited our guests to dine with us and stay the night. It is not safe in the city." His eyes hold a strange light unlike any I have ever seen. "Bring something for them to eat."

I long to tell him to get the food himself, but I hold my tongue.

"Can we meet them, Abi?" Kammani asks, and Ku-aya giggles.

Lot looks at them askance. "You do not know what you ask. These are not ordinary men." He walks back to two men who stand near the window looking out on a darkening sky. From the back, they are impressive, taller than Lot, though even from this distance I feel a sense of fear.

"We have cheese and figs and some cucumbers and melon we can offer," Kammani says, tugging on my arm.

I snatch a different cheese and take the tray with flatbread from a servant's outstretched hands. "I will take it to them." I look at my daughters and bid them to remain behind.

Looking back on that moment, I should have known I would get no sleep, but I could not have predicted the chaos that would come from Lot's simple invitation to those men. The servants returned to their homes before I watched in horror as the men of the city surrounded our house and banged on the door. And Lot . . . How could he offer our girls to those corrupt men just to protect two strangers?

Now I find myself confused and torn by indecision on what to pack after the strangers finally admitted that they were sent by God to destroy our city.

Destroy our city?

I know we live with violence and arrogance, and the morals certainly aren't good compared to what we'd known in Abram's camp. But was Sodom so different than Ur had been? All cities worship other gods, and Abram's God didn't destroy them.

A shiver works through me as a tunic hangs limp in my hand. Why is this happening? Why do I have no desire to do as these strangers insist? Kammani's future husband had laughed at Lot when he'd begged him to join us, as had Kuaya's betrothed. How could we leave them here? What of the promises we'd made, the vows exchanged? Will other men in other cities want our girls, or will we be forced to live with them unmarried all their days?

Nausea stirs my middle, and I let the tunic fall unfolded into a goatskin sack. I should be gathering beans, and we should be loading carts with lentils and pulling vegetables from the garden and loading a donkey with jugs and cooking utensils, as we have done so many times before in our travels with Abram.

Why can I not move? Why can't I push my legs forward or even make a decision? Everywhere I look I see things I want to save, and I cannot fathom the thought of leaving this house I have lived in for so many years. At last we had found a place to call our own, and God would rip it from our hands? Did He think our decision to live here was so bad? We have given our girls culture and music and learning and wisdom from the sacred teachings of our people. We have escaped the uncouth shepherds of Abram's camp. Lot handles those things now or has left them in the capable hands of our shepherds. I am so tired of living in tents.

Is that where I am headed now? Back to living in tents?

A dull ache begins at the back of my neck. I rub it. Take a longing look at my raised bed, something Lot had purchased after Assam's loss. Perhaps there is time to just lie down and rest.

A commotion in the hall causes me to turn too fast. Dizziness sweeps over me. I fling my hands to the wall, grateful for its solid hold.

Lot appears in the arch of the door. "Are you ready?" He looks around, his eyes wide. Wild. "What are you doing? Have you packed nothing?"

I stare at him. "My head hurts." What a stupid thing to say.

"There is no time to think about that." He sounds angry, fearful. "They will make us leave with nothing. You must hurry!"

Leave with nothing? I look slowly around. This cannot possibly be my life. I have a family, we have a home, this is our city, our daughters are to be married . . .

I lift my head. Meet Lot's gaze. "I don't want to go."

"You have to go. There is no choice."

"I would rather die here."

His anger flares, then suddenly cools. "I don't want to lose you, Melah. You must rouse yourself and come. For the sake of the girls. For me and you."

He looks suddenly lost, and I can never deny him when he pouts so. My chest slowly lifts in a deep sigh. "I will try."

Relief fills his expression, and he hurries to the girls' room. I force myself to grab a few more personal garments, stuff them in the bag, and move to the hall toward the cooking room.

But the two men stand there waiting, blocking my way. "There is no more time," one says.

Lot appears beside me, the girls in tow.

"We must go now," says the other.

We are not ready! The words stick in my throat. I hear the girls crying and Lot saying something I cannot quite understand. I need to get the utensils. We need that donkey and at least one cart. We need time!

I feel a strong grip on one of my hands, and the other drops the sack I was carrying. One of the men has taken Lot and me by the hands, and the other grabs hold of the girls. They rush us out the back door toward the hills with instructions to run and not look back.

Not look back? Everything I long for is *back*. Back in Ur and Haran and yes, even Sodom. I would even welcome Abram's camp at this moment. There is no future in those hills. No one ventures to those cities!

My heart beats anxiously, but my feet feel weighted. I hurry on ahead of Lot, the men's command loud in my ears. But all I want to do is go back. To a life I have loved far more than this one can ever be again.

In Our World

Have you ever longed for a time that used to be? I'm not just talking about a do-over because you've blown it in a big way. Rather, are you ever so nostalgic because life has changed too much that you wish you could relive the past? I have.

Sometimes dreaming that the past is better than the present or future is scary. Does that sound strange? Perhaps I should explain.

In 2008, right after my husband and I took a dream trip to Israel, my dad fell and broke his hip. He landed in the hospital, of course, and after surgery to fix things was put into a nursing home for rehab. We honestly thought he would improve and come home again.

But Dad had another condition no one had really thought about that caused him to fear falling again. The pain of that break was too great, and instead of trying to learn to walk again, instead of helping the physical therapist, he fought against him. Even on those days when I showed up to try to encourage my dad's participation, nothing worked. Eventually, because he did not improve, he became a resident of the facility. That was one of the first days that broke my heart.

We did our best to adjust to our new normal. I made it a point to take him food from McDonald's every Wednesday, because years before he was the "McDonald's Grandpa." He loved to take his grandkids and his kids out for lunch, and we were happy to comply.

My dad always appreciated my visits, always smiled wide when he saw me, and gratitude showed in his eyes. I seriously doubt I could ever be that grateful in that situation.

I went weekly because I loved my dad. But nursing homes are not my favorite places to be. If I went in the front door, I had to walk down a long corridor, which included passing many residents who were lined up in the hallways. I recall one elderly woman who sat with a baby doll in her arms and talked about her baby. To this day I don't know if she meant a real child or her doll. Had she lost a child and never gotten over it? Or had she never borne children but wanted to and so pretended she had? I'm sure there are myriad explanations that even skilled doctors can't know for sure, but that woman was living in a different world. Perhaps in a past she couldn't escape. Perhaps in a longing she couldn't erase.

I wonder how often Lot's wife felt that way. We don't know much about her story from Scripture other than she looked back on the cities and turned into a pillar of salt. Why did she look? Was it as simple as a fear that Lot wasn't behind her or that someone was lagging behind? Or was it more deeply rooted in a longing for what she couldn't keep?

I will admit, I'm a sentimentalist. My husband is too. We hang on to things for memory's sake, and I hang on to memories because I want to re-create them. I used to love holidays because they carried similar traditions. At Thanksgiving we often ate the same favorite foods. At Christmas we opened Advent gifts, and Christmas stockings always held an apple and an orange in the toe—a tradition carried over from my childhood.

Gift giving carried the tradition of taking turns and watching each other open presents. We enjoyed Christmas in the morning in our pajamas with coffee cake and orange juice or tea and turned on all the Christmas lights. Sometimes it even snowed on that day, which I considered a special gift from God (even though Jesus probably didn't see snow on the day of His birth).

Birthdays and other holidays included family gatherings and fun decorations and elaborate birthday cakes often hand decorated by my husband or me. Life held fun and laughter and togetherness that is missing now, and we can't get it back, even if we want to.

That's when I understand Lot's wife best. I tend to think she had a hard time letting go, even if she looked back for different reasons. I can understand that sentiment, can't you? Empty nest. Faraway children. My dad in heaven and so much more loss in these intervening years. Loss and grief and fond memories of ages past can make us cling to what once was. And as much as I can relate to that feeling, that longing, and even dream of a day when my family and I might live near each other again, I'm learning that our focus has to be forward, not backward.

Imagine with Me

My breath is coming too fast and my heart beats wildly as I force weighted legs to move, to run uphill. I am not fit to run, and the effort causes me to long to stop. To sit awhile and catch my breath. Is Lot behind me? I can see the girls ahead. I have to keep going.

"Don't look back," the men had said. Why not? What could it possibly hurt to look back on the city one more time? What if Lot has fallen and needs my help? The roaring in my ears makes hearing voices impossible. I will never hear his cries or my girls calling my name. Still, I plod on.

My legs ache and my feet hurt from stumbling over the stones, and I nearly trip on a protruding rock. I cannot believe I dropped the sack with my tunics. What are we supposed to wear when our clothes grow dirty? We brought no coins to purchase anything. Did we? Had Lot thought to keep a pouch of gold coins tied to his belt?

My mind whirls and my head pounds harder from the wine and little food. I should have brought the wine at least. It would allow me to forget this horrible night.

A sigh escapes. I glance to the right ever so slightly. No sign of Lot beside me. I glance left. Again, no sign that Lot is near.

Where are you? But I cannot look back. Fear pounds in my chest until I feel my lungs and heart will burst. What will I do alone with my daughters if I have no husband? If he did not escape the city . . .

And then I hear a roar louder than that in my ears. The smell of sulfur hits me and heat waves waft toward me.

"Lot!" I scream, but hear no answer.

Don't look back. But I cannot stop myself.

From Clinging to Releasing

The apostle Paul said, "But one thing I do: forgetting what lies behind and straining forward to what lies ahead, I press on toward the goal for the prize of the upward call of God in Christ Jesus" (Phil. 3:13–14). He was reaching for the prize that awaits the faithful believer at the end of this life. He saw what was coming and didn't want to go back.

Paul's past wasn't one he wanted to repeat. He'd been a stalwart Hebrew, but he'd also been a persecutor of the Way and a murderer of Christians. He wasn't proud of that fact. He wanted to forget those things because Jesus had redeemed him and set him free from the guilt of his past. God had also shown Paul a glorious future, one that couldn't compare to anything he might suffer here on earth. So Paul's focus was forward, not backward.

Last year as I began to write this book, we suffered several hardships before the year was halfway through. We grieved the loss of family members and faced many new challenges. One thing is true in this life—nothing remains stagnant. We are always moving and changing, and we don't always like those changes. Like the year my dad fell. He lived three and a half years in that nursing home until God called him home. My father-in-law only remained a week in that same place before God called him to His side.

Last year, however, we lost more than we'd ever expected, and if I could take the photos of yesteryear and relive some of those moments, I would treasure them all over again. I would memorize the lines on each face. I would take a mental snapshot to hold close when seasons brought so many changes.

If I could, I would pull out those snapshots and bring them to life again during seasons of change. I would cling to what was because it seemed happier than today. Yet God tells me there is a brighter future coming. A glorious eternity that can't even compare to the best day I've had here!

Why do we find that so hard to believe? Why did Lot's wife want to cling to what she knew instead of embracing a new future?

I think part of the reason is that change is hard. The older we get, the harder change is. When we are young—and I see this in my kids—we are adventurous, spontaneous, excited to live life. But as the years creep by, we don't have quite the energy we once did. Spontaneity sounds like, "How about we plan this instead?" My husband and I took two major trips flying from coast to coast within two weeks because of family issues in 2017, and they were exciting and exhausting all at the same time. Adventure only goes so far as we age!

Yet Paul didn't lose that sense of adventure. He saw what was coming—he was one of the few who was blessed to get a glimpse of heaven. Lot's wife couldn't even see beyond the city she lived in. Sometimes I can't see beyond my own neighborhood. I want to stay put. I'll travel if I have to, but not too often.

However, clinging to what's past, no matter our age, is never a good thing. We don't want to end up like the woman who clung to her baby doll or to dream of Christmases past, which can never be again. We don't want to come to the end of our lives and wish we'd lived better, done the things God gave us to do, loved freely and often, and accepted the path God had for us. Because even if the road is marked with twists and turns we don't quite like, we know a better future is coming.

The past will only drag us down to places we don't want to go—to depression, even mental instability if we let it go too far. The present can be good if we focus on doing the work set before us. And the future will be even better if we know the one who holds it and us in His hands.

Ponder this

When we are tempted to cling to what is past, or to look back and think that what was is better than what is or will be, remember God's promise to Israel, which carries truth for all who believe:

> *"For I know the plans I have for you," declares the Lord, "plans to prosper you and not to harm you, plans to give you hope and a future." (Jer. 29:11 NIV)*

God's plans for us are good, and our future holds so much promise! May we embrace that truth, let go of what holds us back, and keep our eyes fixed on Jesus, who holds our futures in His capable hands.

Taking it further

1. Have you ever looked back and wished you could re-live moments that were especially happy times? How did you handle that desire? What things could you do to help you look back with fondness but move

forward with a spirit of adventure? Have you ever tried to re-create something and found it could never be the same? How did that make you feel?

2. How do you see yourself in light of the past and the future? What emotions do you struggle with when living in memories of the past seems better than a possibly scary future?

3. How can living for the glory of God—living in such a way that you are seeking His plans for you, seeking Him above all else—make today better for you and for those you love? How can keeping a forward focus give you a greater sense of joy today?

6

Rebekah

Doing the Wrong Things for the Right Reasons

(BASED ON GENESIS 25; 27–28)

If I Were Rebekah

The wind is harsh this time of year. Where there are no trees, the sand whips against the skin and cuts like flint. I should be used to these unpleasant seasons, and I know I must venture out of my tent to draw water from the well, but my feet struggle to move. My heart carries the same harsh edge as the wind since Jacob no longer comes to comfort me. How is it possible that Esau's anger still simmers like a pot boiling over?

Isaac no longer blames me for interfering, for he realizes now that it was wrong of him to choose Esau over Jacob.

That he finally accepts God's word to me about the boys still causes me a little thrill of amazement. Until I remember I haven't seen Jacob in years. I thought surely the time would be only a few months.

Jacob planned to travel to my brother, find a wife among his daughters, and return to us, just as Abraham's servant had brought me to Isaac. I never once expected Jacob to remain with Laban so long.

But I could not for a moment consider sending for him. Not yet. Not with Esau raging about the camp like a she-bear deprived of her cubs. What could possibly cause him to hold on to his anger? It has become a living thing within him, and the slightest innocent comment can set his temper ablaze.

A sigh escapes, as it always does when I consider my eldest son. I should have known the fiery red hair that covers him head to foot would reveal an equally fiery personality.

Oh my son, what am I to do with you? The concern fills me often.

Esau's third wife—Ishmael's daughter, no less—does nothing to help matters. As if Esau's two Hittite wives weren't enough trouble! I have long suspected that he went to Ishmael's daughter to console himself after losing the blessing, and in an attempt to please his father. Apparently he thought that marrying a woman from our family line would gain him favor with Isaac. But Isaac and Ishmael have never gotten along.

What were you thinking, my son?

I barely know how to treat his women, and if the truth were known, I avoid them as often as possible. I would rather weave alone than with them. I barely know how to talk to Esau anymore, but that rarely poses a problem, as he is often unwilling to talk to me. He blames me for Jacob's blessing. Rightly so, I suppose, but it was never Esau's blessing to receive.

The wind whips the sides of my tent, and I wrap the edge of my scarf closer about my face. I dread leaving the protection of the strong goat's-hair walls, but I cannot bake or cook without water, and the cistern has grown so low. I must draw from the well, though I wonder if I will be able to make it back up the hill with the heavy jug.

Jacob would have helped me.

A small sob, more like a groan, rises within me. Memories of his laughter and the joy he brought to my life cause my eyes to sting even before I step into the wind.

My son! Oh Adonai, how long?

I have thought several times that the storm had passed, that Jacob could return in safety. We would all live together as families should—in their father's camp. Daughters left their families, but sons remained. How long until I can bring my beloved son home again?

I grab the water jar and brush the tent curtain aside, bracing against the wind. Dawn has barely risen, so I am sure that Esau's lazy wives will still be abed. They never come to the well when I do. Would Jacob's wife accompany me? Had he found someone to love such as I had found with Isaac?

I have not been back to see my brother or mother since I left with Eliezer those many years ago. We've sent word back and forth through the hands of servants, but I have received no word since Jacob arrived three years ago.

Three years. It feels like twenty.

The jug grows weighted in my arms as though I have already filled it. My heart aches as I glance toward Isaac's tent.

He will still be sleeping, as he does so often these days. How long will I have him? And once he is gone, what will happen to me if Jacob still remains with Laban and Esau takes over Jacob's birthright?

Oh Adonai, let me die first.

I haven't entertained such a thought until this moment, but as I walk, head bent against the wind, I realize how little I have left to live for. Without Jacob . . . Would it have been so bad if Esau had ruled and Jacob had married and stayed here? Why had I been so certain that he must not marry a woman of Canaan?

But of course, Abraham had made me see the need of choosing from his lineage rather than from the pagans who live among us. We taught this truth to both of our sons from an early age, but Esau went off and chose two Hittite wives without even consulting his father. Both women have caused us nothing but heartache.

I couldn't bear to let Jacob do the same. But to send him away, all because we had been forced to steal the blessing, all because Isaac had insisted it go to Esau when he knew I was right, all because of Esau's wrath after the deed was done . . .

I've thought often of that moment when I heard the Lord tell me the older would serve the younger. Had I heard wrong? In my exhaustion with the war going on inside of me between the boys, had I heard Him to mean something He didn't?

The well draws closer, and I allow myself a moment to indulge in a memory of Jacob laughing here with his friends, back in the days when he was young and strong and life was good. The wind forces me back a pace, but I push forward, determined now to get the water and return to my tent.

I reach the well and shove away the heavy stone, feeling the work with every part of my body. How old I feel! The rope dangles, and I draw up the bucket several times until the jar brims over. It takes more effort than I thought I possessed to put the stone in place again. I lean against it, digging my feet into the earth to hold myself against the wind. How good it will be when these winds subside and we can return to the predictable weather of sunshine and seasonal rains.

Will Jacob be able to come home then?

I look up, thinking I hear the sound of Esau's wives, but it is only the voice of the wind. I catch my breath. Birdsong flits in the trees overhead, mingling with the sound of rustling leaves. When had life grown so wearying?

Oh Lord, is this the price of bearing sons? To lose them instead of growing old in their presence? Must they be at odds all of their lives?

It was a fearsome thing to be chosen of God. If Jacob had not been chosen, if we could have lived as normal men and women without this blessing—which feels like a curse hanging over our heads these many years—life would have been different. Life would include Jacob.

I lift the water to my head, a task that I have done for as long as I can remember. When did drawing water become a chore? I had always done so willingly, for I enjoyed the task. I brace against the strength of the wind, for it is now at my back, and make my way up the incline to the camp.

Looking back, I see the pride in my knowing. I was right about Jacob. God Himself had told me so. And when Isaac could not be convinced, I had determined that I would fulfill for Jacob what God had promised.

A twinge of doubt pricks my heart as I think on my life while the camp comes into view. Had God needed my help? Might there have been a better way? Would He have intervened if I had asked Him and come up with a plan of His own—one that might have allowed Jacob to stay here?

I stumble, nearly dropping the jug, as the reality of my thoughts hits like a fist to my gut. Had I been so right that I could see no wrong in my actions? Had I risked my son's rule here and now lost him to my brother forever?

Adonai, was I so wrong?

As I slip the jug into its hole in the ground, move into my tent, and collapse on my pallet, I know there will be no answer from the Almighty One. I know the answer already in my heart, and the loss of my beloved son has not been worth it, no matter how right I could have ever been.

In Our World

Have you ever been certain you are right? Not just a little certain, but absolutely sure?

I think this happens to all of us from time to time. I see it in myself and in the world around me. Of course, there is a difference between being right and demanding our rights. For our purposes, I'm not going to address the rights issues because they are too far-reaching and need a book written by someone wiser than I. I'm talking about our day-to-day relationships and our insistence that we are right and we know best!

I'm reminded of the many times I'm tempted to correct my husband's memory. Have you been there? Like the time we traveled out West, one of our many trips over the years, and we got a flat tire in Yosemite National Park. It had been a long day of hiking with the kids and taking in the grandeur of the falls and the huge rocks and the variety of foliage. We were tired and the park was near closing time. We just wanted to get in the van and go to the hotel. But the tire was flat. No way were we going to drive those winding roads out of the park in that condition.

What happened next seemed like nothing short of a miracle. While we were looking around for someone, something, to help us, we looked across the parking lot and noticed a garage. Not like the kind you park your car inside—the kind that fixes cars! So my hubby walked over to see if they were open and if they could help us, and yes they were and yes they could! We were soon on our way with a fixed tire.

We all have such stories, and many times we want to share them. The problem comes in when we—or, rather, our family members—tell it wrong.

My husband could relay the details of that flat tire episode at Yosemite, and he might start out saying, "It happened on a Wednesday at 4:00 p.m." But I am *positive* that it was 4:45 p.m. on a Thursday. He might say the garage was east of the car, and I insist it was west. He might continue to tell the tale despite my interruptions to correct his memory, but after too many times of nitpicking about the details as *he* remembers them, he might grow weary of telling the story and look at me and ask, "Do you want to tell it?"

I'm not sure how many years of marriage it took for me to realize that I was correcting the details of his memory, but I finally decided, *What makes my memory more right than his?*

I could understand if my husband had an issue with remembering things, but he doesn't. And while I might be more detail oriented in some respects, he remembers things that I have totally forgotten. Even if I inscribe those details on my mind, that does not mean I will always remember them correctly.

Time has a way of blurring our memories, no matter how good they are. Even two days later, I'm not going to recall the color of the car parked next to us at Yosemite. In truth, for all of the parks we visited that year, I'm just glad that I still recall it was Yosemite, not Yellowstone. They both start with Y, after all!

These may seem like trivial matters, and they really are unless we allow them to color our relationships. That's where insisting we are right and the other person is wrong can get pretty heated. And in Rebekah's case, doing the wrong thing for the right reason can cause a world of hurt to other people. We can end up seriously hurting ourselves as well.

Imagine with Me

Isaac's hand holds tightly to my arm as we walk to the road Jacob had taken that long-ago day. We're older now, and the distance seems to have lengthened, the time stretching on and on. I strain to see, always hoping, always looking for some glimpse of the dust billowing with his caravan. How I long for him to bring his wives and children to see us so I can wrap them in my arms and Isaac can hold the children on his knees.

Isaac's sight has not improved since that day when we deceived him. He's grown frailer, and I often lie awake at night wondering how long I will have him. But then a strange pain hits me, and I wonder if it is I who will sleep in Sheol first. Most of all, I wonder if we will ever behold Jacob's face again. Once, years after he left, a caravan passed by with word that Jacob still resided with Laban and had two wives. But little word has passed between us since, and Isaac cannot make a trip to visit them.

Still I look at the empty road with no sign of travelers, and after a moment of disappointment, I turn Isaac back toward our camp.

"Not today," he says softly, his voice raspy.

"No. Not today." We repeat the same words as if the repetition itself will bring comfort. If only we could undo the past. If only I had never insisted that Jacob deceive his father and cheat his brother. I never thought . . . I never dreamed the consequences would mean this.

I will die soon. The thought surprises me. Why would I think such a thing? But my heart has lived too long with grief. Being right carries a burden I thought I could live with. I was wrong.

I stumble slightly but quickly right myself as Isaac's hand grips my arm tighter. My mind whirls with too many thoughts. But these weekly trips to scan the road only help Isaac to move his limbs. They do nothing for my heart. I only suffer bruises over what has already broken.

I suppose I should have trusted God more from the start, but trust is so hard! And nothing seemed right back then. Nothing seems right now either. There is no going back, though I have often thought of making the trip to see my brother.

I glance at Isaac. I cannot leave him. And in truth, we are both too old for such a journey.

I wish I had understood these things in my youth. I wish for too many things I cannot have.

From Controlling to Trusting

In my study of Rebekah's life, I saw her as someone who *was* right when it came to what she knew about God's plans for Jacob. God had told her that the older would serve the younger. Esau would serve Jacob. Isaac would pass the patriarchal blessing on to Jacob, who would be ruler of the clan.

Normally, the ruling son was the oldest son. If Isaac had thought for a moment, he would have realized that *he* was not the oldest son of his father, yet God had made him leader in the patriarchal line, which would become Israel and would begin in earnest with his son Jacob. For some reason, Isaac did not see what Rebekah did. The Bible doesn't tell us whether he was there when God told Rebekah about her sons. Maybe he didn't believe her. Or perhaps he just loved Esau more than Jacob, as Scripture indicates, and he wanted Esau to carry the blessing.

Isaac was wrong. Rebekah was right. And she knew it.

The lengths Rebekah went to in order to prove that rightness caused her untold future grief. There is no indication once she sent Jacob off to her brother that she ever saw him again. She thought she would. She intended to call for him as soon as Esau's anger passed. But either Esau's anger never passed or Rebekah died before she could send word for Jacob to come home.

Can you imagine how that must have made her feel? I have three sons, and unlike Isaac and Rebekah, my husband and I don't play favorites with them. We love them all as much as it is possible for a parent to love a child. But as of this writing, all of them have moved to the West Coast while we remain in Michigan.

Now, unlike Rebekah, we have technology that allows us to communicate and even see each other without always having to hop on a plane. But like Rebekah, I don't get to feel their arms around me very often. I don't get to hear their laughter or take comfort in just being in their presence. So I can relate to how hard it must have been for her to trust God as she released her beloved son.

I wonder if she ever rethought her actions or played the what-if game. What if she had not acted as she did? Have you ever wondered what might have happened in their story if Rebekah had waited on God to bring about Jacob's right to rule? It was God, after all, who had told her this would happen. Why not wait for Him to bring it to pass?

But aren't we the same? We might not think we would stoop to deception like she did, but don't we step in front of God's plans and try to force them to happen? Our intentions might be good, but do our methods justify our intentions?

When do we come to the place where we release our children to God's care, when we release whomever we love to Him instead of clinging to what we want for them? When do we stop trying to control the future and let God be God? The one who holds the future, who lives outside of time, can surely handle the things that trouble us. But it's hard to let go, isn't it? It's a lifelong struggle I still face.

Rebekah could have learned a thing or two about waiting on God rather than trying to control and prove her point, but I have to cut her some slack because she didn't have the Spirit of God living in her as we do today. The Bible doesn't indicate that she stopped to ask God what to do when she saw Isaac getting ready to bless Esau. She just did what she thought best. She reacted.

I have to admit, I also react far too often. I've made some pretty good blunders and ruined some relationships because of that. In essence, I think that's one of the lessons Rebekah would teach us today if she were sitting across from us sharing a cup of coffee or a meal of Jacob's stew. I think she would tell us that her stubborn adherence to what she believed had cost her dearly. I can imagine the moisture gathering in her eyes as she talks about Jacob. "You know, my Jacob, he was a good boy. Always did what I told him, even when he didn't agree with me . . ."

In that pause I can hear her say that she wished things had been different. I think of Rebekah as a strong woman and a bit of a control freak. But sometimes our strengths can become our biggest weaknesses.

Where Rebekah was strong showed brightly in her early years, in her adventurous spirit and her love for Isaac. But somewhere along the way that strong personality became one that tried to control her circumstances. In the process, she forgot how to trust.

We don't have to live life having it all together, controlling the minutiae, reacting before thinking, or acting so sure of ourselves. I think Rebekah would tell us that she wished she'd gone to God a second time and asked Him what to do about the blessing instead of taking matters into her own hands. I think she would have looked me in the eye and said, "Trust Adonai, my child. Let Him work out the details."

I just hope that I would listen.

Ponder this

When we find it hard to trust God with what we *know* is right and are tempted to jump in and take control ourselves, we need to stop and remember:

> *The LORD is a refuge for the oppressed,*
> *a stronghold in times of trouble.*
> *Those who know your name trust in you,*
> *for you, LORD, have never forsaken those who seek you.*
> *(Ps. 9:9–10 NIV)*

As hard as trusting may be sometimes, it's the one thing that we can do to show God our love for Him and our faith that He knows best. In the end, He really will work things out for our good, and we won't live with the regret of doing the wrong thing, even if it's for the right reasons.

Taking it further

1. Have you ever ruined a relationship because of an issue of right or wrong? If so, how might you attempt reconciliation? Would people consider you a control freak? What can you do to let God handle the things you can't?

2. Do you think Rebekah made a wise choice in helping Jacob steal the blessing from Esau simply because God had told her the older would serve the younger? Did her knowledge of the truth justify her means?

Why or why not? If you could imagine a different scenario, what might that look like?

3. Do you find it hard to trust God with the future? What steps can you take to learn greater trust that He can control what you cannot? How can believing that God loves you make a difference in the way you trust Him?

7

Rachel

Betrayed by One Who Was Supposed to Protect

(BASED ON GENESIS 29; 31)

If I Were Rachel

There is something about being alone in the fields with the sheep that calms me. I suppose I have always felt thus. They say the youngest in the family always gets her way, but I have never found this to be true. I am sure Leah thinks differently. But then Leah is precisely the reason that I come here alone. She *excels* in baking and cooking and has no use for me there. And while I should be weaving more often and learning more womanly work, I long for escape from my father's house.

I long for escape from Leah.

The sun is high, and the lambs are at rest in the shade of the trees in a meadow near our home. My heart is lighter than in the early days—before Jacob came. But Jacob changed everything, and soon we will be wed. His seven years of service to my father are at an end, and our wedding is only weeks away. At last I will be free of Leah!

Guilt nudges me with that thought. As children we were closer. She was the big sister I adored and followed everywhere about the house. She taught me to spin and a few years later even gave me a lesson in baking her sweetest treats—a recipe she had entrusted to no one else, not even her mother. There was camaraderie and friendship between us, despite our mothers' rivalry for our father's affection. We were two sisters among many brothers, and we knew we had to stick together. But as the years passed and Leah still remained a virgin in our father's house, she grew distant. When Jacob came and wanted me, that childhood closeness dissolved. Nothing I could do or say would bring it back.

A whistle I will recognize until my dying day catches my attention. I look across the field and see Jacob leading my father's flocks, those I didn't shepherd, toward me. His smile grows wide at the sight of me, and I jump up and run to him. He catches me by the shoulders and pulls me close. Oh how I long for his touch!

"Soon, beloved," he whispers against my ear as his lips graze my neck. "Your father has agreed, and soon we will be one."

Heat creeps up my neck as I feel his gentle kiss and hear his tender words so full of promise. We have waited so long!

"I will be ready and waiting," I say, trying to keep the exuberance from my voice.

He holds me at arm's length and smiles. "I have prepared our tent away from your father's house for our use after the wedding week. When you are ready, you may begin to bring your things to make it our home."

That we will live in a tent rather than a house like my father's troubles me, though I refuse to let it dampen my spirits. A tent with Jacob is better than a house with Leah or my father.

I take Jacob's hand and pull him toward the shade to sit with me among the trees. I do not want to think about Leah now.

"I'm sorry I did not have time to build a house for us during the years of our waiting. Your father . . ."

I place a finger over his lips. "I know. He has kept you so busy with the flocks and this chore and that chore that it is a wonder you got any sleep these past seven years." I take his hand again and intertwine our fingers. "I would live anywhere with you, Jacob. A tent will be sweet bliss without the rest of my clan to invade our privacy."

His smile warms me to my toes, and it occurs to me just how alone we are. But I know Jacob to be trustworthy. He will not compromise my virtue even if we are legally betrothed and he is within his rights to shelter me now.

"I would offer a sacrifice to my father's God to bless our union, but I am afraid that I cannot offer one of your father's lambs. I could purchase one, but I fear the cost would be forcing us to wait even longer." He pauses, his gaze intense with love for me. Sometimes it takes my breath.

"I'm sure your God will understand." Would He? I silently pray that He will, though I'm not sure that I yet understand Jacob's faith. My father has always worshiped the household gods. I'm not used to any other, though I have heard Jacob speak of God for seven years.

Jacob nods, but his gaze grows distant. Is he thinking of his home, his family, this God of his father's whom he told me he had met on the way here?

"I am sure you are right," he says at last. He squeezes my hand. "But I must go. There is much yet to do for your father." He stands. "You will return soon?"

I nod. "I'm taking the sheep to the pen behind the house. I will leave with them when the sun dips a little more so the walk is cool. And they will need to drink before we get there."

"I could go with you to the well." His smile brings to mind our first meeting there—the day he said he had fallen in love with me.

"And be late for the meeting with my father?" I stand as well and we face each other, neither one of us wanting to go.

"Of course, you are right. I will water the sheep now and give your father the accounting he is waiting for." A sigh lifts his broad chest. He has worked hard these many years and has filled out from the slender man he had been when he first arrived. "Only a few more weeks."

"Yes." I lean closer and kiss his cheek. "Soon."

"Yes. Soon." He stares at me for a lengthy breath, then calls his sheep and heads back down the hill. I watch him go, my heart singing with anticipation. I can hardly wait for the moment we are man and wife and I will be free of Leah.

Irritation spikes that I should think of her again at that moment. I know she holds it against me that I, the younger, will marry before her, the older. She fears never marrying. I blame my father for not finding a suitable man for her.

She blames me, for it is obvious to all that she pines for Jacob.

I glance at the sky, suddenly impatient to leave this place. I have work to do to prepare for my wedding.

Looking back, I wonder why I didn't suspect that anything could possibly go wrong with my wedding. I lived with a deceptive father and a sister who was in love with my betrothed husband. Not to mention the silent war that went on between Leah's mother and mine. But to lock me away in a room where no one could hear my screams, with a brother who did my father's bidding and held me there . . . If anyone had warned me, I would have told Jacob and run off with him back to his family.

But no one who knew said a word, and even my maid was kept from me. Tears still burn at the memory. I glance toward the hills, waiting as I always do this time of day for Jacob to return with the sheep. Leah and I no longer share a tent, and yet the rivalry between us cannot be greater. Nor the jealousy and near hatred I feel for what she did to us, to me. For what my father has done to us all.

I see Jacob just over the ridge and leave Bilhah to continue with the evening meal. If we were a normal family, we would eat together in community. Leah and I and our maids would work beside each other, and Jacob would share the food at day's end. But I have no desire to share one moment more than I have to of my time or Jacob's with my sister. Let her feel left out and unappreciated. I know it is callous of me to think so, but it was not I who conspired to steal her husband. I am the one who is innocent.

Jacob's smile when he sees me warms me in a way nothing else can, erasing the cold that creeps into my heart each morn as I am forced to listen to Leah nearby, talking with her maid.

I race toward him and jump into his waiting arms. "I've missed you."

His kiss is long, hungry, and I know this answer tells me he feels the same. "You must join me in the fields tomorrow. I have found a spot you will love." His strong arms lift me up, and I am held fast and swung in a circle. "I want to spend the day with you, Rachel."

"And I you." I am nearly giddy with joy over the thought. Could he feel the rapid beating of my heart? "I will gather provisions tonight and we will leave before dawn." How I miss those days with the sheep, but Jacob has rarely taken me since the disastrous start to our marriage.

"I will count on it." He leads me to the pens, and I help him inspect the sheep, pour healing balm over the few with wounds, and count them all. One of my brothers soon comes to spend the night at the pens' opening, while I follow Jacob to my tent for the evening meal.

Tomorrow will be a good day. A day away from the betrayal I cannot escape. If the hurt is not squeezing my heart, I see it in Leah's eyes. I cannot bear to give in to a moment of compassion toward her, sister or not. She had no right to betray me. And I will not let her forget it.

In Our World

I'm not sure anyone in our modern culture can relate to the type of betrayal Rachel lived with throughout her entire married life. Most of us cannot relate to polygamy or to having our father convince our sister to switch places with us at our wedding. But betrayal comes in so many forms, and I bet most of us can understand what it's like to have someone we trusted, someone who was supposed to protect us, abdicate his or her position.

The little girl watches at the window as her daddy pulls out of the drive and waves goodbye, never to return. Maybe he leaves with full intentions of coming back, but his plane goes down or his car crashes or some other tragedy strikes. Or maybe he's walking out on his family because he decided life looked better in another woman's home.

The young husband falls to his knees weeping because the wife of his youth just slammed the door after telling him she no longer loved him. She's done with the life they had built together. She's done with him.

A child dances for joy at the thought of spending time with her grandparents. She's always loved her grandma, and a trip up north sounded like such fun. Grandpa didn't know she'd overheard him say such unkind things about her. *Doesn't Grandpa love me?* The trip goes on with no one suspecting the hurt inflicted on her young heart. What had she done wrong?

Parents come home from church to find a beloved daughter has run away. They had suspected she was making friends with the wrong kinds of kids, the ones they considered rebellious. One of them should have stayed home with her, since she had said she didn't feel well. Frantic, they look for a note, but there is none. Her room is missing some of her clothes and her phone, as though she has just gone to a friend's for a few days. But after days and years of searching, even with police involvement, it is obvious she does not want to be found. Is she alive? Trapped? Hurt? They can't give up, but hope has turned to ash, and they walk around heartsick with every waking breath. *Please, God, bring her home!*

A wife leaves for work despite the nagging feeling in her gut that something isn't quite right with her husband. With their relationship. Had she said the wrong thing again? He'd been so depressed lately, but he can't find a job, and what is she supposed to do? She has to work or they won't eat, but leaving him alone . . . Perhaps she should stay home today. But she knows this feeling, and it has gone on for months. She simply can't take another day away from work just to keep him company.

Oh God, oh God, oh God . . . She should have expected the suicide note.

Pause with me and take a breath. If you have lived through any of these things, even the memory can be jarring. Betrayal is such a vivid form of heartbreak that sometimes I've wondered if you can die of a broken heart. Do you hear my own heart in this?

While the above cases are pulled from real incidents, I have kept the details purposely vague because these things hit too close to home and too close to people I know and love. The truth is, betrayal isn't something we just forget. When someone breaks our trust at such a deep level, we are left with a deep heart wound. When we said, "I do . . . until death parts us," we didn't expect the marriage to end six, thirteen, twenty-five, or forty-three years later. When we had children, we never expected that sweet child to stop loving us. On the flip side, that child never thought the parents who gave him life would abuse him. We all imagine a beautiful family, don't we? We don't expect betrayal to ever enter the picture.

If we take betrayal a step further, we find it grows with each generation. I love history, and I find the time in which my parents and grandparents lived fascinating. My dad spent the early years of his marriage fighting in World War II. I wasn't born yet, but I'm glad he came back or I wouldn't be here today. He spent his time decoding secrets from Axis enemies, trying to catch evil before it happened.

Rachel didn't live with a world war, but I wonder if the war in her home sometimes felt like one. What other world did she know except her family? I imagine there were others living in the community nearby, but how often she got away from the battles with her sister is tough to guess.

Yet there is another side to betrayal that we often overlook: the perception of it when it's not really betrayal.

Hang in there with me a moment. I'm not discrediting any of the serious heartache that true betrayal brings, nor trying to minimize Rachel's or anyone else's pain. Whether this type of disloyalty is real, as in a broken marriage or ruined relationship, or perceived, as in a wounded heart because of a misunderstanding gone too far, both can feel like betrayal, and we lose trust in those we feel deceived us.

But sometimes we can feel wounded by someone we trusted when that person never meant to hurt us. They never actually walked out on the relationship. There was no verbal or physical abuse. No intentional unfaithfulness. Yet we can misinterpret another's actions so easily, can't we? I know I can. I've done it so often I would still feel ashamed of it except for the grace of Jesus.

Rachel didn't misinterpret her father's or sister's actions. They directly affected her. But later, in the years she was forced to share her husband, there might have been moments when she felt abandoned by Jacob just because Leah kept getting pregnant and she couldn't. It was not Jacob's fault. The Bible indicates that God had kept Rachel from bearing children (Gen. 30:2, 22).

Have you ever felt betrayed or abandoned by God? He was silent in Rachel's cries for a child. Had she done something to deserve what her father and sister did? The way Scripture reads—and I suspect in her mind—she must have felt like she was being punished simply because Jacob loved her. Would you blame God in such a situation?

I think if we are honest, we'll admit that any type of disloyalty brings with it the temptation to blame. We are hurt, we are wounded, and we can't understand why these circumstances are happening to *us*. If we aren't careful, blame turns into grudge-holding with deep roots of bitterness. And bitterness will eventually destroy us.

We get a glimpse of the grudge Rachel held when many years later she dealt her father a mighty blow. Their relationship was never the same because of his actions and her reaction to her situation.

Imagine with Me

My heart beat hard the night I snuck into my father's house and stole his household gods. Jacob had insisted it was time to leave, to return to his father, and Leah and I had for once agreed. But despite Joseph's birth—at last, vindication and a child of my own—my sense of bitterness had not abated.

You could say I hated my father, pompous, proud, deceitful man that he was. And taking his gods would wound him. I wanted to hurt him as he had hurt me.

Thinking on it now, I wonder why I let such bitterness control me. For after I took them, I felt this immediate conviction that I was wrong, and when he came looking for those silly gods, my heart had softened. If not for Jacob's vow to kill the person found with the gods, I would have returned them. They were of no use to me. And indeed, I was ashamed of my rash actions.

I buried them later and forgot about them, though sometimes I wonder if God truly forgave the bitterness I'd carried for so long. It had eaten at me, and sometimes I struggled to show Jacob the love and joy he needed from me because of it. Bitterness has a way of crowding out love.

I do my best to push it aside now and live the life I've been given, though it does creep into my heart now and then, especially when one of Leah's sons says something unkind to Joseph, or Jacob spends time with Leah because I am unclean. I hate that he is ever alone with her. Even now the sharing of him stings.

I wonder if I will ever be free of these feelings. It was not my fault I was betrayed by those who were supposed to protect me. I have every right to blame them and hold it against them. But somehow I know that I need to forgive and let go of the pain.

I am just not sure I know how to do so.

From Wounded to Forgiving

If you have read any of my novels, you know that the theme of my stories, of my life, is forgiveness and reconciliation. After all, one who has been forgiven by a loving God wants to bring about that same reconciliation and love to everyone else. I can't help the desire to share Jesus any more than I can stop breathing. I recall sharing Him in my childhood and in my teens, and I still do so in my life thus far.

But forgiveness can look far different to a child than to an adult who has seen the harshness of life. We all live with our own suffering, our own pain, and none of us can claim that our pain is worse than someone else's because we can't know that person's heart. Only Jesus has that ability. As God told the prophet Samuel, "People look at the outward appearance, but the LORD looks at the heart" (1 Sam. 16:7 NIV).

I couldn't look into Rachel's heart even if she and I were in the same room, sharing our life stories. I can only read about her circumstances and imagine how they might have seemed to her in her culture, which I explored in my novel *Rachel*. After all, the human heart and the emotions we feel don't change with time. Only our culture and circumstances do.

Still, betrayal in any culture carries vast implications and consequences. A mom doesn't walk out on her family and expect to just walk back into the lives of her children, fully accepted, twenty years later. A man doesn't give up his neighbor to a ruthless regime and live without paying for his actions in some form or another. A person doesn't cheat his family out of their inheritance and imagine that he will ever have a healthy relationship with them again. Betrayal brings consequences, including pain.

Rachel suffered a terrible blow when her father forced her to wait to marry Jacob. Even if she and Leah had been sister-friends, once they had to share a husband and Rachel was denied children, she would have felt like an utter failure in her culture. While she had Jacob's undying love, the deceit skewed her emotions, and her focus became a jealous bout of rivalry with Leah that lasted years.

There is no mention of forgiveness in the biblical story on any level, although we can speculate that Leah and Rachel eventually became friends. But stop and think about this for a moment, if you will: Could Rachel have forgiven her father without restoring their relationship, assuming they had a relationship worth restoring? Some parents just aren't close to their kids and don't want that closeness. If it were me, I would want that. I loved my dad. I miss him more with every passing year. But I had a good relationship with him from the start, and he would never have put me in Rachel's position!

Because of that good relationship I had with my dad and mom, the great marriage I have, and the kids who have blessed our lives, I always thought that any relationship could be mended if both parties were just willing to try to understand each other and forgive whatever hurts still remained. But I also know that Scripture says, "If it is possible, as far as it depends on you, live at peace with everyone" (Rom. 12:18 NIV). We can't *make* other people live at peace with us or forgive us. We can't make other people love us or even like us! We can't control anyone or any circumstances. We can only control our own reactions—and sometimes I struggle to control mine. Don't you?

I can also control my choices, good or bad. And I've learned that we can go from feeling wounded by the actions of others to forgiving by choice. If we choose to forgive, then by God's grace, we can forgive. That doesn't make it easy. Far from it. Sometimes I have to beg God for grace to forgive the same thing over and over again because the memory still causes pain.

While we can forgive, we can't always reconcile. If you think about it, there are a lot of things that we just can't get back. That divorce and remarriage happened and we can't go back. We can forgive the spouse who abandoned us, but we can't reconcile by having a relationship with them again.

Abuse, both verbal and physical, happens far too often, and it leaves lasting scars no matter how we look at it. Hopefully we can forgive, but we may have to step away from any type of relationship with that person lest we open ourselves up to the abuse again. God never asked us to submit to abuse. He said we might be persecuted for our faith, but that's not the same thing. A mom who knows her man is beating her child needs to protect that child. Otherwise she is betraying the child just as much as the abuser is.

When my dad was dying I asked him for a memory from his childhood. His short-term memory wasn't so good. But without hesitation he pulled up a memory of doing something wrong as a child. He didn't have to spell it out for me to know that the memory stuck because of how his parents reacted. I can't prove my dad was abused, but his comments even with a compromised state of memory were telling. All because he damaged a material possession when he was a little boy. Material possessions can be replaced. Little boys' hearts can remain scarred even into old age.

Did my dad forgive his parents? I'm certain of it. But he didn't have a close relationship with them. We lived too far apart and there was too much history I'll never know. But my dad was not a man to hold a grudge. He too was some-one who knew forgiveness, and he loved Jesus. He went to his grave at peace with all who would be at peace with him.

And when it comes down to it, that is how we move from feeling betrayed or wounded to forgiving. If we have been forgiven for the wrongs we've committed against others—and none of us can skip that part because we are all guilty on some level—then we can also forgive. If we trust in Jesus, we know that forgiving others is a command. It is also a choice.

I will never minimize the hurt that is attached to betrayal. Betrayal destroys our dreams. But in some of the cases above, I've seen the one deceived, abandoned, or betrayed turn those feelings into exactly the forgiveness of which I speak. Some have even gone so far as to pray for the one who wronged them. Reconciliation may not be possible, but godly love from a distance can be.

No one, especially me, is promising this is easy, and it's something each person must work out for themselves. But with God there is hope. God, who can calm the stormy seas, is also very capable of calming our turbulent emotions and healing our hurting pasts—if we'll ask Him.

Ponder this

When we are faced with betrayal on any level, remember the psalmist's words about God:

> *You are my hiding place;*
> *you will protect me from trouble*
> *and surround me with songs of deliverance.*
> *(Ps. 32:7 NIV)*

The Lord can deliver us from the pain of betrayal or abuse. He can give us a heart willing to forgive as we have been forgiven. When the memory no longer causes pain, we will know a sense of great freedom. And God will surround us with songs of deliverance!

Taking it further

1. Have you ever been betrayed by someone who should have protected you, someone you trusted? How did you deal with that person and the situation afterward? If that pain still weighs heavy on your heart, what can you do to find peace?

2. Do you think Rachel held a grudge against her father or her sister? Do you think she could have forgiven either one for the way they treated her? How might you have felt if you could have walked a moment in her sandals?

3. Do you ever feel like God has let you down because of the circumstances you've been forced to live with? Can you go to Him with the feelings of hurt and anger and give them to Him? Do you believe it is possible to forgive, even if you can't see the relationship restored? Why or why not?

Leah

A Risky Chance at Love

(BASED ON GENESIS 29)

If I Were Leah

Dusk deepens as I step into the courtyard, listening to the conversations of my father and brothers. They do not notice me where I stand along the wall. My father has already had too much to drink, and my brothers are arguing about Jacob.

"You really do need to honor his request, Father."

"*I* think he should return to his father with nothing."

"Father made a bargain. He cannot go back on his word."

"Jacob has made you wealthy, Father. He knows how to care for sheep, even if he isn't good at much else."

Laughter follows, but my heart has already stirred at the mention of his name. *Jacob*. This cousin who came to us seven years ago and lost his heart to my sister Rachel.

The realization stings, though I have tried all these years not to let it. Surely a man will want me soon, my father has assured me. Over and over I've heard the words. But he does little to find such a man to take me as his wife.

The wind lifts the scarf from my face, blowing it gently behind me. I grasp it and pull it back to hide beneath it, but the men do not notice.

"So Jacob's seven years are up," my father says, affirming what has already been said, his words slightly slurred. "And he wants to marry Rachel. Not Leah. Even when I showed him how good she cooks. Still he wants the youngest." He waves a hand in frustration, and my heart aches at his words. They are true, of course. Jacob has flatly ignored my father's attempts to show off my talents.

Murmurs of understanding accompany my father's statement, and my heart sinks as I recall the look I saw pass between Jacob and my sister at the meal. The joy so evident in her eyes that at last their union would come to fruition. They had waited so long, she'd said in a heady moment on her way to her room. "At last," she crooned.

She knows nothing about waiting. My sister is young and foolishly in love with a man older than she, even older than I. But at least I have had the years of training to be a wife, the years to learn how to manage a household, while Rachel runs around with the sheep. The girl knows nothing, and yet they will give her in marriage and let me wilt on the vine?

My heart twists with familiar pain. No one wants me. My father would be rid of me, for I am becoming a burden except for my weaving, and Jacob will never consider me when beautiful Rachel fills his vision every waking moment.

No one loves me or wants to get to know me. And my father has done nothing to set things right. What man in the village is even free to marry? What passing traveler could be coaxed to stay and take me on as his wife? I would be a burden and a struggle to any husband my father could find. I know I would because I am afraid.

Yes, that is the truth of it. I can't look at men the way my sister can because of fear. They say my eyes are weak. But it's timidity that makes me unable to show the confidence a man wants in a woman.

I am plenty confident. Give me wheat and water and dates and figs and wine and I can create almost any tasty morsel. Give me flax or wool and I can create linen or baskets or weave tapestries that belong in kings' palaces. But give me time alone with a man and my tongue grows thick and my thoughts elude me. I'm not even sure I could make more than casual conversation with Jacob, despite my feelings for him.

How easily Rachel seems to be able to speak to him. Sometimes he is actually amiable to me and responds with genuine kindness. I remember once when I greeted him because Rachel was confined to her room during her time, and he smiled and we joked about the lamb that had wandered off. He'd had to chase after her, nearly getting himself stuck in a small crevice while trying to get her out.

Once they are wed, will he speak to me like that again?

"We can't let Rachel wed before Leah," my father says, jolting my thoughts to the conversation once more. I press my back harder against the stones of the house, wishing I could melt into the room beyond.

"So what do you propose we do, Father?" my oldest brother asks. "You can't make Jacob wait. He has already served the time you agreed to."

I watch my father pull on his pipe, the aroma filling the courtyard, making me almost light-headed. He exhales and leans back, looking from one brother to another. "I have decided to give Jacob what he has earned, but he will not necessarily like it." He laughs long and loud, and I cringe at the sound of it. What is so completely humorous at a time such as this?

"Leah, come out from the shadows," my father commands suddenly.

I nearly jump out of my skin. I had not thought they'd noticed me.

I move slowly forward and come to kneel at his side. "What is it, Abba?" Though he has never deserved the endearment in my opinion, I offer it anyway.

His smile holds a calculating edge. "Your sister. She is in her room?"

I nod. "I believe that is where she was headed."

My father looks at one of my brothers, who grudgingly stands and moves into the house, probably to make sure Rachel is indeed inside. At this hour, where else would she go? She is planning and dreaming of her coming wedding. Something I have also given thought to, but only during the times when I secretly weave my wedding garments in hopes that my father will act one day.

Never mind that I have wanted Jacob from the first day he arrived here. Never mind that I have woven the garment for him. Now I will never wear it.

But as my father begins to tell me his plan for me to switch places with Rachel under the cover of darkness and the veil, promising me that he will fill Jacob with enough strong wine that he will not know the difference until morning, my heart fills with the strangest eerie longing. I had hoped for this. And my mother had intimated the possibility, hadn't she? But to hear my father lay out the plan . . . I feel almost faint.

"What if he recognizes me before he fulfills the night? Rachel and I are similar in size, but we are not the same. He could cast me out and I would be ruined!" I say the words in a whisper, for fear of reprisal. What if Jacob heard?

"He will not recognize you, my daughter, and he will not throw you out." My father is not thinking clearly.

"You cannot know that."

"I will do all that I can to ensure it." He smiles my way and pats my hand. "Do not worry, my Leah. You will not be shamed into living without love while your younger sister gets everything you deserve."

I stare at him, my heart doing little flips. Oh, how I want to say yes, to agree to this plan. But to take such a risk for love? What if Jacob never loves me? Worse, what if he hates me for what I do? I cannot live with that.

And yet . . . I cannot live without trying.

In Our World

Have you ever taken a huge risk? As I write this, I'm sitting on a heating pad nursing a perpetually troublesome backache. To say I'm not in the mood for any type of risk at this moment would be an understatement. But then, when I think of risks, I often think of daredevil stunts like the kind we see in movies, especially before CGI became popular.

I remember taking our kids to Disney World many years ago, and one of our favorite shows, still popular today, was the *Indiana Jones Epic Stunt Spectacular!* One of our sons wanted to watch the show over and over, and we actually talked to one of the stuntmen afterward. My son decided he wanted to become a stunt performer when he grew up. As his mom, I'm rather glad he didn't choose a lifestyle with those kinds of risks.

While raising our boys, I heard about all kinds of things they considered trying. Bungee jumping. Skydiving. Walking on water. Well, maybe not that last one. And the others I kindly asked them to wait to do until I'm no longer around. Perhaps they will do these things and just tell me afterward, but the risk doesn't thrill me. Some people thrive on such things.

Other risks like public speaking, which I'm told is one of the most feared things other than the dentist, don't bother me. I like my dentist and I like to speak as long as I know what to say. Still, to a lot of us those things pose a huge risk. We risk exposure. We risk making a fool of ourselves. What if the audience doesn't like us? What if the dentist hurts us?

I'll admit, speaking to a group of women and watching one of them sleep through your talk also risks your pride. A speaker can tell when an audience isn't engaged, and they can feel like an utter failure for not entertaining them. But let's face it, not every speech is going to come off perfect. Pastors make simple mistakes and they speak every week, sometimes multiple times a weekend. It can be distracting to see people get up and leave or fall asleep, but it's a risk speakers, teachers, and leaders of every stripe take.

Whether we realize it or not, we all take risks nearly every day. It's risky to reach out to a new friend or group of friends. In the past ten years, our kids have taken big risks—cross-country moves, new jobs, marriage, parenting, starting a business.

Just loving someone is a risk because we put our hearts on the line, and what if that love is not reciprocated? Like with Leah.

When I think about Leah donning those veils and pretending to be her sister, I wonder how fast her heart pounded. Did she want to jump out of her skin when Jacob spoke to her? What if he found out? What if he exposed her to ultimate humiliation and cast her out?

Some risks are dangerous for more than the obvious reasons of physical security. Whether we act like we are invincible by climbing a mountain without a tether or inject illegal drugs into our bodies, we have to know at some level that we are risking death. Ignoring pain or illness can also be foolishly risky. And lying to get what we want can be equally foolish and risky, even if we aren't found out.

Leah's risk for a chance at love was found out with dawn's breaking light, and she paid for her deception for the rest of her life. We can speculate that Jacob came to care for her in some small way because she gave him sons. We can also speculate that after Rachel's death, Jacob became more attached to Leah. But she spent years fighting the same battle she'd fought before she agreed to do her father's bidding— that is, warring with her sister. I don't know about you, but I would not have wanted to take that chance. Of course, in her day, life would have been far worse for her if she had never married, so perhaps she weighed the odds and determined the risk was worth it.

I think the bigger question for us as women today is, are we taking risks that go too far?

Have you ever gotten to a place in life where you felt like you've waited too long, life just isn't fair, you want answers now? Our journeys don't always turn out the way we envisioned them, do they? Most of us do not live the perfect life we would have chosen if all of the decisions were up to us.

But we don't get to control the things that make us wait or cause us to feel like life is passing us by. We can reach for the golden ring and miss, then spend years wondering where things went wrong.

In this risky business of life, we are going to make some choices that are good and some that are not. A lot of things are going to happen to us or around us that shape the way we think about people, the world, ourselves, even God. The temptation is to ask that ultimate question, "Why?" Or, more honestly, "Why me?"

I have a feeling Leah and Rachel both had that question cross their minds. Why did their father use them against Jacob? Why did Rachel's sister betray her? Why didn't Leah's husband love her?

Even if they knew the answers, it might not have been enough to stop the questions. Unfortunately, "why" questions rarely have satisfactory answers. But in our frantic desire to understand, we can make dangerous assumptions and act in ways that make matters worse. We can ruin relationships by trying too hard to fix misunderstandings. We might hurt our reputation, our job, our families, and our walk with God because we want answers and are tired of trusting Him.

Can you hear my heart when I say this? Have you ever felt like you had to chance something to get what you wanted, because you couldn't believe God really had what was best for you in mind? I have. While I didn't experience the desperate feelings Leah may have had for a husband, I have felt them in other aspects of living. Waiting is so hard, isn't it?

For the young woman who feels like life is passing her by, doesn't it seem reasonable to just accept any opportunity for love that comes along? Or maybe give up on love altogether?

For the sake of Leah's story, I'm more inclined to empathize with the many young adults I know who are still waiting, still longing for that one person to share life with. How long do you search? Do you marry a guy because it seems like time is running out?

In some cases, risks like that can be huge mistakes, as I believe Leah came to see in years to come. Though she might have loved Jacob, Jacob did not return her love. He had eyes only for Rachel, and until her death he may not have paid Leah much notice. Can you imagine being married for years in a loveless relationship? Some risks aren't worth taking.

But if you're asking God to lead and guide you into a godly marriage—if that is His plan for you—then you are risking faith in God, not in yourself, yes?

Love involves faith in God to lead us to the person He has planned for us. And it also involves faith in that person to keep our heart.

And that's what it comes to with true love. Love is a risk in itself because we offer our hearts, knowing that someday they might be broken. When we have to say goodbye because this earthly life has ended for one of us, there is no getting around the grief love risks.

Can God be trusted to give us the love we crave? Are we willing and able to risk our hearts and let Him lead us to where we are meant to be?

Imagine with Me

The hills are brown, and though the sun shines, my heart carries a gray wisp of loss that time has never been able to erase. Jacob hobbles over the fields in the valleys below the hills. He tells me he is checking on the sheep, on his sons. But I know he simply wants time alone. Away from those sons, the ones I gave him.

Rachel's Benjamin is the only one who brings him pleasure now. Joseph is dead. Rachel is dead. Dinah is defiled, as good as dead. And Judah has abandoned us to live with the Canaanites. There was something in that boy's eyes that made me wonder. He fled out of guilt, though he would not tell me why.

And now I hear rumors from the gossips at the well that Judah has taken a wife and she has borne him three sons. Sons I have never held on my knees. Grandsons Jacob has never seen. *Judah, my heart, when will you come home?*

It seems so long ago now that my father sent me to Jacob's bed on Rachel's wedding night. I had thought that in time Jacob would love me. The birth of Judah, my fourth son, had even brought praise to Adonai to my lips, for I knew even without my husband's love that the risk had been worth it. God had seen that I was not loved, and He had blessed my womb. How I had rejoiced in that child's birth!

So much has come between us since. I had hoped the loss of Rachel would draw Jacob to me. But he spent most of his time with Joseph and Benjamin. He rarely shared my tent. Only a meal now and then when the boys were spending the night in the fields.

Jacob. How long I have loved just the sight of you. And yet even now I know that I am barely more than a companion. Someone he can talk to who isn't a child to be trained or taught, despite the fact that his sons are now grown men. It is not the same with children. For that one reason, I think, Jacob seeks my company now and then.

Life is not what I expected, even though I am glad to have wed and birthed children. I did not expect the pain, the struggles, the loss, the heartache that come with age. That come with loving a man who does not love me in return.

Would I do it again?

I glance up at the sound of footsteps. Jacob, walking toward me, leans heavily on his staff. His eyes are shadowed, his beard gray, but it is the pain in his heart that emanates from him with every step he takes. His wounds since Joseph's loss have never healed. And I will never be able to fill the hole Rachel's death has left in him.

For that reason I wonder if it truly was worth the risk. I should have been mistress of my own home with my own husband. I know that now. I think even God might have been pleased with that arrangement.

But I cannot undo what is past, and I know I will never make Jacob love me as he did Rachel. I rise, brush the dust from my skirt, and move closer to meet him just the same. He is all I have now, and whether he can give me what I want or not, I know our God can give him what he needs.

From Risk to Faith

Leah came to know Jacob's God at some point in her life. Many people point to the praise she offered God upon the birth of her fourth son, Judah, as evidence of her faith. Until his birth, the names she picked for her sons all reflected an aching desire for her husband's love, not God's.

Leah's risky chance at love led her to find a love she didn't expect in the grace of her husband's God. Her father's gods were figurines that were enshrined somewhere on her father's property. Figurines can't love, nor are they worthy of the praise Leah gave Adonai.

Does that mean Leah made the right choice? What would have happened if she had married another and Rachel and Jacob had ended up in a monogamous marriage like Jacob's father had? Some might wonder where the twelve tribes of Israel would have come from if not for the four women in Jacob's family. But that thinking says the end justifies the means.

From the beginning God intended marriage to be monogamous. Children are His heritage. If I could rewrite Leah's story, she would have married another. Rachel and Jacob would have had as many children as God allowed. Joseph's story would have ended differently. Egypt, the exodus, might all have been different.

The point, though, is not to rewrite history. We cannot in our finite minds figure out how things would have been different in the trickle-down effect if Leah had not taken that risk. Was it God's plan that this deception happen in her life?

While I believe with all of my heart that God is sovereign, deceit is never condoned in Scripture. God does not orchestrate sin. He redeems us from it and brings good out of it for those who love Him, but that does not give us license to make poor choices, lie, take foolish risks, or sin in any way.

God can create something good out of nothing, so He can definitely create something good out of our messes and our messed-up world. One day He will make all things new—better than we could ever imagine. But wouldn't things have been better for Leah if she had waited and trusted God to the end? I imagine the reward she would have found would have far outweighed her years of strife.

The thing about Leah's risky chance for love is that it took untold years of heartache, tears, jealousy, and so much pain before she reached that place where she could accept faith. Where she could accept forgiveness for what she'd done. Where she could truly know love.

And isn't that true of all of us? None of us comes to faith without recognizing we need God. As long as there is something blocking our ability to see that need, such as Leah's deceit did, we will fight against anything to do with faith. We won't be able to see past ourselves to take the risk that faith needs. The right kind of risk that leads us to the greatest love of all.

I believe that once we have taken that biggest risk—where we surrender our hearts to God and trust Him and His timing—there will be times when God will ask us to take even more risks. Like Peter stepping out of the boat to walk on water. Like Mary being labeled an immoral woman when she agreed to God's plan for her future as the mother of the Christ. Like George Müller starting an orphanage with no money and trusting through prayer alone that God would provide. Like Kent Brantly risking personal health to minister to sick and dying people in Liberia who had contracted Ebola.

Like those risking safety to rescue human trafficking victims in our own cities or lost children on the streets of India.

The list is as endless as the world has needs. God often calls His people to risk their comfort for the sake of the cross, for the sake of sharing His love with the world.

But taking a risky chance at love or any other pursuit in life that is primarily self-serving? God doesn't ask us to risk something that goes against the purpose of His will. He asks us to trust Him with our hearts' longings and wait for Him to act.

Does that mean He will never bring us into a situation for love or a job or a friendship that won't include risk? No. I think our God likes to mix things up a little and give us new reasons to trust Him. That might mean trusting Him as we walk alone into that new church in that new town where our job has transferred us. It might mean going to a friend's house to meet someone who turns out to be pretty special, maybe even the guy we come to love.

Perhaps if Leah had lived in our time and not had to depend on her father to find her a mate, she would have found a friend who understood her and arranged for her to meet the man who would have given her that love she craved. Still, the lesson is the same. Abraham had learned it generations before Leah's time: Wait patiently and trust. Risks don't always turn out so well, as he learned with Hagar. But faith won for both Abraham and Leah in the end, even if they did learn the hard way.

Part of that learning comes in changing the question from "Why me?" to "What do You want to teach me, Lord?" or "Where do we go from here? How do I handle this part of the journey, this time when I want to risk the wrong things because I don't want to wait on You?" Learning to ask God the right questions when our circumstances aren't going the way we'd hoped could help us to differentiate between taking a chance to trust God, even amid the risk, and rushing ahead of God into a risk we will regret.

Risks might take faith. But faith determines whether the risks are worth taking.

Ponder this

When life makes us feel unloved, even unlovable, and we are tempted to take foolish risks to feel good about ourselves, remember God's promise to those who know Him:

> *See what great love the Father has lavished on us, that we should be called children of God! And that is what we are!* (*1 John 3:1 NIV*)

As God's daughters—children of the King of Kings—we have the privilege of bringing our needs, our desires, to Him. He has already lavished us with the greatest of loves when He gave us His Son, Jesus. Sometimes He might ask us to wait for Him to answer some of our hearts' longings, but His purpose for us is always wrapped up in a Father's perfect love. We are His beloved, and no one and no circumstance can take that away from us.

Taking it further

1. Have you ever longed for love but discovered it was impossible to find? How did that make you feel?

2. What kinds of risks do you take? If you know you are risking things outside of what God has for you, how can you change your perspective? What might you do to help you trust God to lead you?

3. Can you trust God with what He has planned specifically for you, whatever that may mean? How does Leah's life teach you that some risks might not be worth taking?

9

Dinah

Choices That Change Everything

(BASED ON GENESIS 34)

If I Were Dinah

The late summer breeze tickles my face as I stand near the edge of the land where we dwell. The grapes are in the other direction, and I sent Adi there ahead of me. I just want a glimpse. One look toward the city. I can hear the festival music even from this place where I hide among the trees. Young women my age will be there. Dancing. Singing. Laughing.

My heart longs to move closer. To see with my own eyes what Simeon and some of my other brothers have described with wild interest. Why is Ima so worried? They are girls like me. Surely a city will be a safe place. What could possibly go wrong?

Irritation toward Ima's warnings spikes as I creep closer to the road that leads away from Abba's camp. It would probably be wiser to take Joseph with me, or Issachar or someone I could have coaxed away from the fields. But Abba had sent them all off to care for the flocks, and if I wait, the festival will be past. I will miss my best chance to meet the girls all at once. On a normal day, most of them would likely be working in their parents' homes.

My feet move of their own accord toward the heady music. I glance behind me. No one follows, not even Adi. Good. I need time away from all of them. The camp has grown stifling in recent months, not from the heat, for we are well protected by the trees, but from Ima's hovering. Her fear. And her constant reminders that I should wed someone soon.

I don't want to wed someone yet. I have years left if I wait as long as Ima and Aunt Rachel waited to marry. Why is she so worried that I marry younger than she did? Besides, I know no one in the camp who captivates me. They are un-interesting or can't take their eyes off me. A clammy feeling creeps up my spine at the memory. I don't want to marry a man who looks at me as if he can see beneath my robe!

But to hear Simeon talk, all men are the same. A wife is simply a person to beget sons for her husband and care for his needs. I don't want to be like that, like Ima and Abba. I want what Aunt Rachel has with Abba. Someone who speaks words of love to me and who holds me as if he does not ever want to let me go.

A sigh escapes as the longing rises within me again. Is there no one for me like there was for Aunt Rachel? If Abba had been given his way, I would not even be here. Ima would have married another, and who knows what children she would have borne? The thought has often troubled me, for I wish my parents loved each other like Joseph's parents do. But Abba seems incapable of loving anyone more than Aunt Rachel.

I want more. Better.

I cinch my scarf closer to my neck, and my heart trips with a mixture of excitement and trepidation. I can do this. I can sneak into the city and return before Ima knows I'm gone. Let Adi gather grapes. She won't tell. And I can sit at dinner tonight with the secret of knowing I have done something I have always wanted to do and all is well. I can prove to Ima that her fears are wrong.

I glance behind me again and step onto the road, my gait hurried. With my decision made now, there is no use holding back. The closer the gate looms, the lighter my heart feels. What fun this will be! The music entices and beckons me. The guards at the gate do not stop me, though I feel slightly uncomfortable with the looks they give me. Just like the men in the camp. Can none be civil?

I follow the music to the center of town, where a large crowd has gathered in the marketplace. Men watch as young women dance in the center of a large circle. My heart pounds as the shouts of the men nearly drown out the music. I slip into one of the merchant booths and hide, but a woman calls to me. Before I can deny her, she has sold me one of the colorful scarfs with a sheer veil, like those that flow loosely behind the dancing girls.

"You are not from around here," the woman says, lifting a brow.

"No. Yes. That is, I live outside of town." I feel my nerves heighten as the crowd grows louder. The neighing of a horse catches my attention, as though it is being held at the reins and wants to break free. I understand the feeling.

"You're from that group—the men of Jacob." The woman peers more closely at me, and I take a step back, saying nothing. "Are you here alone? No men are with you?"

Why is she asking me so many questions? Suddenly Ima's warnings flash in my mind. But no. It is silly to worry. The woman is simply being friendly.

I smile. "My men are watching the crowd," I say, silently hoping Abba's God will not strike me for the lie. I am protecting myself, after all.

The woman nods and smiles. "So they have come to snatch a bride from among us? Or perhaps they are just curious onlookers."

"They are just curious." I take another small step back. "I really should join them. They only allowed me to come so I could see the shops and meet some of the young girls."

"You won't likely meet the girls today," the woman says, her brow furrowed. "This is when the poorer virgins seek a husband. They don't chatter and gossip like we do at the well. They are too busy trying to catch the eye of one of our men."

"Oh, I see." Disappointment settles hard within me. I had not thought that meeting the girls would be impossible above the noise or the crowds. I should not have come. But I force a smile and move closer to the door. "I'd best join my brothers." I hesitate a moment as I try to find a way past the men blocking the door.

"Come this way." The woman stands behind me and takes my arm. I flinch, and she loosens her grip. "I mean you no harm, miss. But if you take this side door, you can find your brothers, and the gate is closer."

I meet her gaze. I wonder if she knows I'm not being honest and is doing her best to protect me. I follow her and slip into the city, slightly away from the crowds. I glance at the scarf in my hands and quickly tie it over my pale blue one. The veil hangs over my eyes, though I can still clearly see. Then I move swiftly toward the gate. The music causes my feet to lift slightly, and as I move through the gate, free at last of the crowd and my fear of the men, I cannot help but laugh and dance in a quick whirl. I have done it! I have come, and I am safely away from the city now.

I dance and twirl again, echoing the song I can hear the women singing in the distance like chants, over and over again. What would Ima say if she saw me now?

I stop. How will I explain the scarf? Remorse fills me. I should not have wasted precious silver on something so frivolous. Perhaps I should bury it, despite the joy the colors bring to my heart. I can hide it in my tent. Ima won't have to know. I pick up my pace and determine to remove it when I grow closer to camp.

My ears perk at the sound of a man's whistle. Footsteps draw closer, and I glimpse a man dressed in fine clothes walking toward the city. I step to the side of the road, but he has seen me. I look back, then forward. I can't go back, and he's blocking the road home. I search the trees lining the road. If I run toward them, can I escape into the underbrush? I hurry toward them, but my legs feel weighted. I rip the scarf from my head and toss it aside.

Footsteps, heavy and strong, rush toward me. I can't move fast enough. But I *have* to get away.

My breath comes hard, and fear brings bile to my throat. *Ima!* I can't scream, and she isn't close enough to hear me anyway.

A strong hand grabs me from behind. "Ah, caught you! Thought you could escape, did you?" The cultured voice holds the edge of one who has just won a great prize. His grip tightens as I struggle to get away.

"Let me go!"

He laughs. "That's not how we play the game, little one."

His arms come around me, and he carries me deeper into the woods despite my kicking and screaming. He seems amused by it all. Does he think me one of the women of his city?

The scarf flashes in my mind, and I fight harder. "Let me go! I am not one of your women! I am Jacob's daughter, and you will be sorry if you do not release me at once." How bold I sound.

"Jacob's daughter? The Hebrew?"

"Yes! Now let me go!"

His look grows serious as he tosses me down among soft grass and pins my arms to my sides. "I don't care whose daughter you are, little one. I am the prince in this city, and now you are mine."

In Our World

Do you ever wonder why Dinah wandered off alone to a place she didn't know? In a sense, she reminds me of a runaway—an unhappy young girl who feels trapped at home for whatever reason and sees something better just around the bend or in the city out of reach.

Even if we aren't runaways in the literal sense, I wonder how many of us are runaways at heart. How often do we think about leaving, starting over, changing our circumstances? If statistics are true, it seems like escapism, the desire for something *else*, is rampant in our land. Even in our churches. It might explain, at least in part, why the divorce rate is so high. Serious reasons like abuse and infidelity aside, sometimes we just get bored with life, don't we? And even if we don't do something as drastic as divorce, we might move or change jobs or look for a new group to join. Restlessness seems to be a common trait we all must face from time to time.

Perhaps we are the son or daughter who was raised in a conservative home, and we step into the world and want to taste what it has to offer. Like Dinah wanted to step away from her father's camp to taste the life of the city that practically stood on her doorstep. She wanted friends. Are you sensing how she might have felt?

Like most girls, she just wanted to fit in with girls her own age—or at least meet them. Can't fault her for that. Unfortunately, she didn't think through her decision very well, and she paid the consequences for the rest of her life.

Someone once told me that there are different types of friendships. Some people are in our life for a season, but life changes and they, or we, move on. Others are acquaintances. We know each other, but there is no closeness, no actual trust beyond the superficial.

Still others might be business friendships that only last as long as we are working together at work, school, church, or in community service. They're temporary relationships. I think that's the kind of friendship Dinah might have been looking for—just someone new to talk to. I rather doubt she thought she would make a lasting friendship with people who worshiped other gods, with girls who didn't share the values of her family.

What she needed, as we all do, was a close friend. Someone she could confide in and share girl secrets with and laugh with and who understood her, who listened to her. Most girls don't find that with their moms—unfortunately for us moms—especially when they reach the age where they could start their own families, as Dinah could have done had she not been caught in such devastating circumstances. And while the Bible mentions Jacob's clan having daughters that might intermarry with these city people, Dinah is the only one mentioned by name. Dinah is the only daughter of Jacob that we know existed.

Now, it's possible that Jacob had other daughters and that Dinah is only mentioned because of what happened to her. So Dinah might have had sisters, but even a sister isn't always a good friend, if Leah and Rachel are any example. Dinah wanted more. She wanted a friend she wasn't related to or who didn't serve her. Or maybe she just wanted to see for herself what other girls did with their lives. Was their life more exciting than hers?

Aren't we like that too? We want to know, to see things, for ourselves. We want the experience personally, not vicariously. It's way more fun to travel to see the mountains or the canyons or the ocean than it is just to see them on TV. Who wouldn't rather experience a roller coaster (or a more tame ride) than just hear about it?

Most of us want to feel alive, to experience life to the full, but sometimes we can't—not at the time or in the way we'd like to. Perhaps physical limitations or age restrictions or people standing in our way stop us from fulfilling our dreams, but that doesn't mean they can take those dreams from us.

The thing I think about from a biblical perspective is, are we longing for the right things? Are we chasing something that could harm us? Are we longing for something that God has warned us to avoid? We balk and wrestle and fight what is best for us, because no one likes to be told what to do. Even Christians. We struggle with listening to God because sometimes He seems like He just wants to keep us from having fun or doing what we want to do. The desire to have our own way is as old as time.

And Dinah was no different. But the consequences she lived with the rest of her days . . . well, I wonder if she ever regretted her choice that day.

Imagine with Me

My hands are wrinkled now, worn with work, scarred with trying to scrape away the pain I can never quite erase. We moved to Egypt years ago, once Joseph called us to come, but that's a story for another day.

Joseph. How I missed him while he was gone from us. He would have comforted me, actually did try to comfort me after what Levi and Simeon did. Would it have really been so bad to let me stay with Shechem? I know what he did was wrong. So wrong. But then he spoke such loving words to me, and he took me into his house like a new bride. Who else would have me anyway? I was badly shaken, to be sure, but I could have made a life with him. I would at least have had a family of my own then.

But after Simeon and Levi killed the men, even the girls of the town wouldn't speak to me. The friends I'd sought, captives of my brothers after that awful day, hated me. Blamed me for everything. Was it my fault? Shechem was the one who had harmed me, so why was I the one shunned?

The shade is hot under Egypt's midday sun. No one works when it grows so warm, and I can hear the snores of some of my brothers taking a rest from their labors. Their sons care for the sheep now, and Joseph—he doesn't live near enough to spend time with me as he did when we were young.

Young. How foolish I was then. And yet . . . after that brutal attack, Shechem had shown me the kind of love a man has for a woman—at least that's how it seemed—for the next few days. He couldn't stop himself from his great longing for me, couldn't make himself wait until my father gave his blessing. And I believed him.

But I also knew my father was never going to give his blessing. Deep down, I feared Ima had been right all along, and while I wanted to be loved as Shechem showed love, I knew it was wrong. And I knew I would never escape this man who held me captive with his words and his insatiable desire.

In my wiser moments, I realize that Shechem's actions toward me were never as loving as he wanted me to think they were. But I didn't expect him to die for what he'd done. Nor in the midst of those swirling emotions did I ever imagine I would never know a man again. Never marry. Never feel the strength of a masculine hug or the whisper of intimate words.

I tell myself, as I gaze at the stars in this foreign land or look on my aging brothers, that nothing matters anymore. My life will soon end. And my choices will die with me. I'd like to think I've done some good for others along the way. That my life, single and childless, is not in vain.

But sometimes my imagination leaves me wanting.

From Loss to Acceptance

We cannot know for certain whether Dinah ever married after her tragic encounter with Shechem. In our culture, it has become more acceptable than it was in years past for a woman to sleep with a man outside of marriage. In Dinah's day, it was scandalous. And rape was a violent crime, as it still is today. I have no doubt Dinah grieved, not only because she was brutally accosted but because she knew she would likely never marry. In her culture, she would not have gotten past the scorn for another man to want to marry her. While there were some exceptions, as in Rahab's story, marriage to someone who had lost her virginity was the exception, not the rule. Virginity was so highly valued in those days that proof of virginity was given to the father of the bride, should the groom ever try to say he'd married a woman who was not completely pure (see Deut. 22:13–19).

Dinah suffered a great loss in her day. Some might look at the passage in Genesis and wonder why Jacob didn't just give his blessing and allow her to stay with Shechem. Yes, he had violated her, but he was also offering his protection for her, and since her prospects had just tanked, it might have actually seemed like a good idea. The law of Moses (to come much later) made provision for this very thing: "If a man seduces a virgin who is not betrothed and lies with her, he shall give the bride-price for her and make her his wife. If her father utterly refuses to give her to him, he shall pay money equal to the bride-price for virgins" (Exod. 22:16–17).

Jacob did neither. He said nothing while his sons did all of the talking and deceived Shechem, intending to kill every male in town. Dinah, who at this point was still in Shechem's home, was removed by her brothers and lost any hope of marriage. At least, that's one way of looking at it.

It is possible that Dinah was given in marriage to another at some later date. The Bible does not say, nor does it mention her after she moved to Egypt. What we can know is that she suffered a great tragedy and loss. She lost her virtue, her most precious possession. And she lost her future as she hoped it would be.

Can you relate? Have you ever done something or had something happen to you that utterly changed the course of your life? Life can change in an instant, can't it? When we least expect it, we can be faced with the most trying of circumstances, and our lives are never the same.

Those moments can not only destroy our dreams; they can also make us bitter people. Life rarely goes the way we expect it to, and most of us don't get to live as we intended. A day will come when we must choose to let those circumstances make us stronger or weaker, better or bitter. We can choose to blame every future sorrow on the past or learn from what we cannot change.

Looking back, I can think of several times in my life when I was blindsided by the unexpected. Things I never dreamed would happen did. Trials and heartache I never expected came anyway. I had a hard choice to make. I could be like some people I know and grow deeply bitter, consumed by the hurt. Or I could learn to live out grace and forgive.

Let me say that forgiving something like Dinah went through would take a supernatural act of grace. Maybe she did forgive. But when someone abuses us or deceives us or hurts us beyond anything we could have imagined, forgiving them does not always include trusting them again. Sometimes we can, in time. The woman who cheats on her husband might be able to win his trust and forgiveness and they might save their marriage. The addict who gets clean can be trusted again if he wants to remain clean and never forgets where he's come from. His life will not be easy, but he *can* change by God's grace.

This isn't always the case. And for a rape victim like Dinah or anyone who has been physically, sexually, or verbally abused, I would not expect that person to trust the abuser again, despite apologies or wooing words. I think Scripture gives us Dinah's story but leaves out the details of her later life perhaps because the focus of the incident was her brothers' actions rather than her feelings. Only God can someday tell us why we never learn her thoughts on the matter.

Empathizing with her plight, I know how hard it can be to move on with life when something capsizes our ship. When we feel like we're drowning, we need a life preserver, and fast. We need rescue and then we need help—someone to listen, to counsel us, to pray with us. We need grace. Grace to forgive. Grace to discern whether to trust again. Grace to accept the unacceptable and keep living, keep breathing, without letting ourselves be swept away in a sea of anger and hatred and vengeance and poisonous thoughts.

I've watched bitterness destroy people. I've heard the angry words that never seem to stop. And I've said a few of them myself in those trying times. But when God has ahold of our hearts, He has a way of working in us, shaping us, loving us, and helping us to find grace in our times of deepest need.

I've had my share of arguments with Him along the way when dealing with grief and loss. Like Jacob, I'm a wrestler at heart, but I never win when I wrestle with the Lord. He's too good at reminding me how much I've been forgiven and how willing He is to give me the exact grace I need to forgive, let go, bless, and love. Even though. Even when. Even through the hardest of times.

I hope Dinah found a way to forgive her attacker, her brothers, and her father, and accept forgiveness for herself for walking away from safety to pursue a foolish choice. Her life would have continued pretty miserably if she hadn't. She could have ended her days a sick, bitter old woman. I hope that was not her life.

I hope that is never my life or yours. Have you been there at some level? Have you ever had to make the choice to accept your mistakes or your sins and repent of them and turn back to the truth that God is there for you? He loves you. Have you felt His grace giving you the strength to do the impossible when accepting terrible loss? I pray so. I'm learning that the more I come boldly and ask for His grace to do what I cannot, the more He gives it. I just have to give up my hurts and let Him have them, and learn to live in spite of my bad choices.

Ponder this

When life hits us with the unexpected and we are left reeling or mourning or lost and confused, remember how very much God has given us in Christ. Because of the cross, Jesus now intercedes for us as our High Priest, and the book of Hebrews tells us,

> *For we do not have a high priest who is unable to empathize with our weaknesses, but we have one who has been tempted in every way, just as we are–yet he did not sin. Let us then approach God's throne of grace with confidence, so that we may receive mercy and find grace to help us in our time of need. (4:15–16 NIV)*

Never be afraid to ask for grace. God is always willing to freely give us exactly the help we need to get through something, to forgive, to keep moving forward. Trust Him.

Taking it further

1. Have you ever made a foolish choice that ended up costing you far more than you could have imagined? What happened?

2. If you have lived through trauma like Dinah did, how did you handle it? When you have been hurt by the world, have you been able to forgive those who caused you pain?

3. Can you let God give you the grace to get past whatever tragic thing it is that clings to you and wants to steal your peace, your life? What can you learn from Dinah's experience?

10

Aneksi
(Potiphar's Wife)

Desperately Trying to Fill the Emptiness
(BASED ON GENESIS 39)

If I Were Potiphar's Wife

The air in the room drips with the scents of myrrh and aloe and human flesh, and though I lean against the wall near an open window to relieve my senses, this annual gathering of Pharaoh's guards wearies me. Potiphar struts about the room, his square chin tipped up, his laughter grating. When had I tired of hearing his voice?

The other women, wives of the guards, make a point to seek me out, to sing my husband's praises, to make it clear how grateful they are to have their own husbands chosen to work for the man. I nod politely and offer a stiff smile.

"How happy you must be to be married to such a fine leader as Potiphar," one young, overly adoring wife whispers close to my ear. Her breath smells of the rich wine Potiphar has supplied, and I take a step back. As his wife, I am expected to keep a respectable distance, despite my role as hostess of this pompous charade.

"Yes, most happy," I respond as I turn my back and listen to two other women tell of the latest gossip from the palace courts. Their husbands stand guard in Pharaoh's audience chamber. Now and then they have something to tell beyond the latest boring cases of law or trade.

"I've heard that Pharaoh may forgo his annual gathering this year," one says, her hand fanning her face despite the cool breeze coming through the window off the Nile. "They say he has been plagued with threats to his life because of the recent taxation decree."

"Not to mention the added building projects he has placed on the workers. They are already forced to work beyond what used to be expected." The other woman leans closer to the first, and I strain to hear. "It is treasonous to say so, but the workers, the people, have reason to be angry. But would they really rise up against Pharaoh?"

The conversation intrigues me until the two women begin to speculate about things of which they cannot know. Pharaoh is well guarded, if Potiphar's words can be trusted, and I know my husband well enough to know that he works long hours to ensure our king's safety.

I walk across the room, our largest receiving room where these banquets are held. Pharaoh's parties are so much more desirable than ours. It will be a disappointment if he cancels this year's gathering because of a simple threat. Potiphar's feast cannot match that of Pharaoh's, despite the expense and choice wines. I look around, longing for something to distract me. When had my life grown so restless? The best things in Egypt surround me, and yet . . . I glance down at my manicured nails. The henna patterns used to make me smile with a small sense of pride. The garments and wigs and tapestries and furniture that Potiphar allows me to choose had once delighted me and fulfilled my sense of need. I had purpose.

What a fool I had been in those early days of marriage. Perhaps if I had borne a child . . . I shove the thought aside. Nothing can change that now, for either I am barren or Potiphar is incapable of quickening life within me.

I look up and let my gaze travel the room. Musicians take up one corner with their soft strumming of harps and lyres, while a juggler entertains those who care to watch. Male servants move about the room, carrying trays of food and a variety of drinks, all of them purposely avoiding me per my wishes. I cannot risk Potiphar knowing how well acquainted I have become with his handpicked slaves.

My name, Aneksi, means "she belongs to me," and Potiphar made certain from the moment we wed that every male who works near our home or in the fields or under his military command knows that I am his.

"You're mine now, Aneksi," he had whispered among the pure white linens of our marriage bed. "None but mine." He'd made the words sound pleasing then, and in my naïve youthfulness, I thrilled to his protectiveness. The strongest, greatest man in Pharaoh's employ called me his. I was heady with the sense of such belonging. He had noticed me, and I meant something to him. Unlike the way I'd felt growing up in a houseful of beautiful sisters.

When had the protectiveness turned to possession? "You are mine, Aneksi. Never forget that." His tone had grown threatening the one time he had seen me gaze overlong at one of the handsome male servants.

I learned to mask my desires after that. I even try to win my husband's affection and lure him to my bed every chance that I can. But Potiphar seldom returns home from the palace early and often stops at the gaming houses or, from what I have heard, visits some of the women of ill repute. Why? Am I so lacking all of a sudden that he must cast me aside for a prostitute? Is he punishing me for a simple look?

I set my jaw at the memory and walk, head high, across the expansive room. Potiphar sits in a corner with some of his men, telling one of his foolish tales. I brush past and continue to walk back and forth across the room. It would serve the man right if I pulled one of the servants aside even now and took him from the room to my bed. Let Potiphar think I still play his little hostess. He is too besotted with food and wine and his own self-importance to notice. But of course I will not. Not now. Not this way.

I smooth sweaty palms on the soft linen of my narrow shift and lift my chest as I move close to one of the servants I had told to stay away. I hide a smile at his look of fear. I have learned it is wise to keep them all from thinking they hold anything over me. For all of my brazen acts, it is they who will suffer most. I might be divorced or imprisoned, but they will die. I glance knowingly at the man before moving on. I am not so callous as to want a man to die on my behalf.

I do not stop to think why the thrill of control I have over these men is one of the few things left that brings feeling to my heart. Not a good feeling. But I ignore the threat of conscience. Feeling *something*, good or bad, is better than feeling empty . . . or worse, nothing at all.

The drone of the party sounds like an incessant drum in my ears. I move to the doors and step onto the porch overlooking the Nile. In the distance the houses of the servants stand small and silent. No one sleeps this night except for the field hands.

I squint into the darkness, past the torches that line the wide porch. One field hand in particular comes to mind, and my pulse suddenly quickens at the thought of him. Potiphar purchased him recently from a band of Ishmaelite traders. A Hebrew. Joseph.

Now *there* is a man worth knowing. A man who will surely bring more than the bitter feelings of that need to control to my heart. I sensed something different in him the moment I laid eyes on him. More handsome and stronger than any of the servants in Potiphar's employ, Joseph also carries an air of near royalty about him. It seems preposterous to see royalty in a slave, but in the short time he has been here, Potiphar has already begun to sing his praises. Everything flourishes under Joseph's hand.

Suddenly the party is not nearly so boring as I begin to imagine what Joseph will be like compared to the many other servants who have discreetly shared my bed. I rub my arms to ward off a delighted chill, now acutely aware of what I must do. I will work to bring Joseph to serve in the house and then tempt him with all of the things I can offer. Potiphar need never know why I desire another servant. Perhaps it is time to send one of the others to the fields in exchange for this perfect specimen of a man.

I turn from gazing at the fields and the houses of the workers and return to the party, my step light with purpose.

In Our World

Potiphar's wife. I think she must be one of the most difficult women in Scripture to understand. Or to relate to on a personal level. Then again, if you've seen the movie *The Graduate*, you could consider Potiphar's wife as the original Mrs. Robinson.

Sin in the hearts of men and women is nearly as old as dirt—literally. Though we don't know how long Adam and Eve lived with God before sin destroyed their relationship, we do know that once it did, desires that rebel against the nature of God have flourished. Time has not changed those desires or improved them. Oh, they may take new forms and appear as something new, but the original enemy of our souls is still the same, and he's not very creative. Thus Mrs. Potiphar and Mrs. Robinson. Same idea. Same sin of adultery. The only difference between the two might be their motivation. What led each woman to seek sex outside of her marriage? In the movie, we can guess at Mrs. Robinson's boredom and attraction to someone younger. Was this the motivation that plagued Potiphar's wife too?

Adultery is a sin and is equally as hurtful as any immoral act or expression. Maybe it's worse, because it's coming from someone who promised to love us until life's end. And when that person steps outside of those marriage bonds, it's betrayal. Those of you who have been there know what I'm saying, yes?

Even if we try to redefine marriage from a covenant for life to a contract that can be broken (yes, that's some of the popular thinking today), either way sex outside of marriage is still adultery in God's eyes. And adultery is not a private sin, though it is often done in private. It reaches beyond the devastated spouse to the children, the extended families, the friends, the coworkers, even the neighbors. When Jesus said, "What therefore God has joined together, let not man separate" (Mark 10:9), He meant it for a reason.

Although we may be tempted to place the blame for adultery mostly on the men, let's remember that this chapter is about Potiphar's wife. She was the one with wandering eyes. Proverbs warns against the adulterous woman, though men have probably gained more notoriety in this equal-opportunity sin. Even in Scripture there is no more famous story of adultery than David and Bathsheba. David, the man after God's own heart, went after the wife of another man, just as Potiphar's wife went after Joseph. Except she didn't have the power David had, and she didn't get what she wanted. Still, none of us are exempt from immoral thinking or immoral behavior. Potiphar's wife had both.

I gave her the name Aneksi for the purpose of these fictional scenes. As I searched for ancient Egyptian names, Aneksi's apparent meaning, "she belongs to me," seemed to fit how I saw her relationship to Potiphar. In Scripture, however, she is nameless, and to some extent that makes her seem almost invisible. Not to Joseph, of course. He couldn't get away from her fast enough. But I wonder if she didn't feel invisible in the life she was forced to live. And if we feel as though no one sees us, doesn't that make our lives seem empty? I know I feel that way.

When I walk into a new setting and don't know a single soul, I can fade into the woodwork or just listen quietly. I can also reach out and be friendly to those around me. But when I walk into a place where people know me and yet act as though I'm not there, that hurts. Or when my calls go unreturned or I find myself always last in line and picked last for the team. There are many, many ways to feel forgotten, overlooked, invisible, empty, nameless.

Like Potiphar's wife.

She probably had an arranged marriage, and though she landed in a prosperous house with a wealthy, well-respected husband, for whatever reason her life had grown lonely or boring or meaningless. Should we blame her husband for her lack?

I'm not here to cast blame on anyone, particularly the victims of adultery, because many times there truly are innocent parties who did nothing to deserve the way they were treated. As in the case of Uriah in the story of Bathsheba and David. Uriah was innocent and more honorable than David. So it's entirely possible that Potiphar was honorable like he was.

But sometimes there is neglect or abuse, or there are other circumstances that cause husbands and wives to grow distant and their love to grow cold. I have to wonder in this case if Potiphar's wife was feeling a chill from her husband as the years went by. Was he too busy at work? The Bible indicates the only thing he had to concern himself with once Joseph took charge was the food he ate. Interesting that Scripture focuses on only that one thing. So Potiphar didn't concern himself with his wife?

But who was overseeing her? Who was committed to her above all others? In Joseph's opinion, God valued the marriage covenant, and he wasn't about to break up his boss's marriage. Perhaps Potiphar valued his marriage too, though I wonder if he could have been a little more attentive to his wife. There is no indication that he was cheating on her, only that she wanted to cheat on him. We also do not know whether she had slept with other servants. That part comes from my imagination, so please read the story in Scripture for the truth of what actually happened.

One thing is certain—the takeaway lesson from Potiphar's wife is,

> Above all else, guard your heart,
> for everything you do flows from it. (Prov. 4:23 NIV)

Have you ever been caught in a place where you were tempted to do something you shouldn't? Did you find yourself in a battle for your heart? I think every one of us faces such temptations at some point in our lives. If the man after God's own heart could fall into such temptation, what makes us think we are stronger, better? First Corinthians 10:11–13 tells us,

> Now these things happened to them as an example, but they were written down for our instruction, on whom the end of the ages has come. *Therefore let anyone who thinks that he stands take heed lest he fall.* No temptation has overtaken you that is not common to man. God is faithful, and he will not let you be tempted beyond your ability, but with the temptation he will also provide the way of escape, that you may be able to endure it. (emphasis mine)

None of us are exempt from the feelings that overcame Potiphar's wife. It's what we do with them that can make the difference between her and us. Between her fate and ours.

The guy at the office had charmed her, made her feel like she was beautiful, and no one had made her feel that way in a very long time. But she hadn't planned for dinner to go beyond that. He was simply being nice, and with Mike away . . . why not? The kids were grown and off at school, and Mike traveled so much.

She still felt guilty when she thought of Al, but that temptation to meet him again . . . she couldn't seem to shake it. Day after day he filled her thoughts with his honeyed words, and at night when Mike wasn't there for her anyway, Al had a way of making her forget her husband of twenty-three years.

Before long, her thoughts grew to obsession, and she began to seek him out. What had started with his obvious interest had mushroomed into her constant desire. All they needed was to each get a divorce—she from Mike and he from Cassie. The kids would understand. They could see how lonely she'd grown, how distant their dad acted. Couldn't they? All she had to do was make Al see what she saw all too clearly.

I'm guessing we've all heard similar tales too many times, even in our churches. Any one of us can be tempted to think the grass is greener in somebody else's yard. In my forty-plus years of marriage, I've seen infidelity happen to countless couples, and there doesn't seem to be any slowing down of the desperate grasp at immorality in this country. We just find different ways to express it.

Very few people, though there are some, "run from any-thing that stimulates youthful lusts" (2 Tim. 2:22 NLT) as Joseph did. Of course, Joseph might not have had any prob-lem fleeing. We aren't told that *he* lusted. Only that *she* did. If she was anything like Mrs. Robinson, he might not have found running away from her difficult until she made it im-possible for him to resist her any other way. The Bible tells us that when Joseph fled, he left his garment behind.

I'm not exactly sure what the Bible means by "garment." In Israel, Joseph would have been used to wearing a tunic and a robe and later his coat of many colors that set him above his brothers. (Which was part of what got him sold into slavery in the first place.) But in Egypt, they weren't quite as covered. It was a warmer climate, or perhaps they didn't mind display-ing the human body—kind of like the difference between the swimsuits of the 1920s my grandmother wore, which covered most of her skin, and the string bikinis of today. There was a big difference in how much the eye could see.

As a slave, did Joseph wear a simple covering, like under-wear or shorts? Or as an overseer, did he wear a tunic-type garment with perhaps a cloak or robe? Whatever it was, it was proof that Potiphar's wife could show to her husband and make whatever accusation she wanted against this man who had scorned her advances one too many times. Can you imagine how she felt? True, she was the one in the wrong. But if she felt lonely or neglected by her husband and then was shunned day after day by her husband's Hebrew slave, might she have grown angry? The wounds she may have wanted to deal to her husband fell on her. She was the one feeling let down and rejected, whether those feelings were justified or not.

Imagine with Me

It seems like a lifetime ago since that day I stood on the porch of our house and dreamed of enticing the Hebrew Joseph. My jaw clenches tight at every thought of that upstart, arrogant *slave*.

He sits in prison now, an unjust punishment for his crimes against me. If Potiphar were truly my protector as he once claimed, he would have hung the man! But no. Potiphar had become too enamored with the Hebrew during the years it took me to work up my nerve and my plan to bring Joseph to my bed. The plotting and planning had been like sweet wine to my soul, especially on those nights when Potiphar did not come home, when he entrusted everything to Joseph's care and stayed long at the gaming house or with his men, running military practices for Pharaoh. I lost patience with him long ago.

A bird twitters outside my window, and I rise from my couch, fighting a stinging sense of rejection, of a loss I did not anticipate. When had Joseph become my obsession? When had convincing him to lie with me consumed my every waking moment? Is my life so dull, so meaningless, that I have had to resort to such frequent faithlessness?

Potiphar could have had me killed if he knew. Though more likely he would have sent me back to my father or put me out on the street.

Did he know?

A shiver works through me as the memories plague me yet again.

"Lie with me," I'd said when I caught Joseph in the house, going over Potiphar's accounts. Other servants roamed about, but they had all been to my bed or knew those who had. They also knew that one word to my husband would be the end of their employ, if not their very life.

But Joseph was not so easily swayed, as the others had been. His words that first time still ring in my ear. *"Because of me my master has no concern about anything in the house, and he has put everything that he has in my charge. He is not greater in this house than I am, nor has he kept back anything from me except you, because you are his wife. How then can I do this great wickedness and sin against God?"*

God. Which god? We worship everything from the Nile to the sun to the cat, and many more creatures we are certain protect us. And how dare he call my desire "great wickedness"! I am not wicked.

The thought bristles, and I pace the spacious bedchamber even as I snap at my maids to leave me in peace. Peace. What a perfectly foolish concept. There is no peace in Egypt or Potiphar's house, and most especially not since my husband has sentenced Joseph to prison. The king's prison, not the one that holds commoners.

Potiphar knows.

I stop midpace as a sick feeling pours through me, turning my limbs to liquid. I spent years planning and days pleading with the Hebrew, and in the end my husband believed the Hebrew more than he did me. And worst of all, Joseph would not give in to my desire, despite everything I did to show him all that could be his if he would but listen to my plea.

He did not care for you. No one cares for you. Potiphar keeps you to make himself look good, but he does not love you. If he truly cared, Joseph would be dead and Potiphar would come back to you instead of spending his time on other women, in other places.

The thoughts plague me, growing daily in strength until I think I might go mad. It isn't true. The servants care for me. My friends care. Even Potiphar cares in his own distorted way.

It is Joseph's fault I am in this state. If he had never been brought into this house, I would not have been tempted to seduce him. If he had been a decent man, he would have given me what I asked.

"It's not my fault," I repeat to my aching head and heart. I sink onto the plush couch and call for a servant to massage my feet and bring me food. There is no need to leave my chambers. Potiphar has already left for the day. Joseph sits in a prisoner's chamber.

And I sit in a prison of Potiphar's making.

Of your own making.

No. Not my own making. I am not wicked. *I* did not choose this life. I am not the one who will face the devourer and have to give an account for this mess. Potiphar and Joseph—they will pay.

Somehow that thought brings little comfort.

From Rejection to Denial

Rejection is a powerful emotion. To feel unwanted or shunned cuts deep into the core of our being. It attacks who we are at the most basic level. It defies our value and negates our worth. Have you been there? I have.

I'd like to say the only rejection I've felt has been during my twenty-year attempt to sell my books to a publisher. But that type of rejection, hard as it was to bear, is nothing compared to rejection from people I know or love.

The rejection I felt for twenty years was more like being turned down for a job over and over again. Did it hurt? Absolutely! Such dismissal can cause any of us to feel as though our work has no worth. We must not be good enough. Someone is always better than we are at what we long to do.

But compare that to the mom who runs away from home and doesn't return. What does that devastated dad say to his son and daughter when they come home from school and find out Mommy isn't coming back?

Or consider the grown-up daughter who decides she doesn't want anything to do with her dad anymore. Or the son who leaves home strung out on drugs, never to return.

These are generic scenarios, but they happen to real people every day. We know the people affected. We *are* the people affected by the choices of others.

Rejection in any form hurts, but it doesn't simply hurt the person it is intended to. A man or woman who hates another distresses everyone around them. An unforgiving person's bitterness poisons the very air he breathes until he becomes toxic.

Potiphar's wife was toxic to Joseph and to her husband by cheating on her man—or trying to. I can bet that Potiphar's household was well aware of her antics and certainly not blind to her schemes. We think we can hide our sin—Adam and Eve tried to do that right from the start—but God is not deceived and He can't be mocked. What we sow, we reap. And unfortunately for Joseph, Aneksi's actions caused him a blow that sent him back to captivity instead of the relative freedom he had begun to enjoy.

Do you think she took responsibility, told her husband the truth, repented of what she'd done? There is no indication in

Scripture that she did so. If she had, Potiphar could have lifted Joseph out of prison and restored him to his former workplace. But his wife would have suffered for her honesty—or could have—and so she cast blame where it didn't belong.

Do we do that? Cast blame instead of accepting blame? It's so easy to do, isn't it? We had good teachers in the first man and woman, and now blame seems to escalate faster each day, each year. The only time someone apologizes or admits to wrongdoing seems to be when they are caught in their sin, when they can no longer intimidate or deny the truth that the problem stems from their inner being—*our inner being*—not someone else's.

We live in a flawed world, and the truth is, we are a broken people. It doesn't take a degree in psychology to show that we are not perfect either in thought or in action. Some of us might think we're good because we would never do something as bad as what Potiphar's wife or even King David did. We would not cheat or murder or lie or deceive.

Yet can any of us really say that with a clear conscience? We may try. I know people who live year after year denying the very things that keep them from finding freedom, purpose, and wholeness. The things that keep them from knowing Jesus. They would rather live in denial, stuffing bitterness into that empty hole in their hearts, keeping anger as a weapon to use against those who might dare try to help them see the truth about their attitudes or actions. Instead of seeking God and finding acceptance in Him—in Christ—and entering into His family, some would rather run from Him and deny that they are capable of wrong. And they lose the joy and peace of knowing how much God loves them. They miss the chance to have Jesus fill the void that keeps them blaming others for their own circumstances or feelings or, in some cases, even their choices.

How might Aneksi have fared if she had looked at Joseph in a different light? If instead of becoming enamored with his good looks, she had wondered about his belief in one God? Her story in Scripture might have been entirely different.

God used her deceit and treachery ultimately for Joseph's good, but the story didn't end so well for her. She is never spoken of again and remains in history as a nameless wife of Potiphar.

Her story is a lesson for all of us. There will come a day when we may be tempted to do what she did, or something completely different but with similar empty consequences. But the temptation to do something is not the same as actually doing it. God made a way for Joseph to escape, and He would have made a way for Aneksi to escape her immoral desires if she had asked Him.

There will be trials in life that may take us down, bring us to the breaking point. Those are not the same as temptations, which will also come. But while God may not give us a way out of trials, He promises to make a way of escape when it comes to being tempted to do wrong (1 Cor. 10:13).

We don't have to give in to immoral cravings as Potiphar's wife did. God knows our weaknesses, and if we let Him, He will help us overcome life's biggest temptations.

Ponder this

When we are tempted to think life is meaningless, remember that God can fill the empty places in our hearts. We are not nameless or forgotten. God sees us. He knows the struggles we are facing.

> *God's solid foundation stands firm, sealed with this inscription: "The Lord knows those who are his." (2 Tim. 2:19 NIV)*

We need never give in to the hopelessness Potiphar's wife may have felt. We have a Redeemer. A Savior. And we will never become a nameless woman of history when we are His.

Taking it further

1. Have you ever felt an aching emptiness inside, in a place no one but you can see? When have you been tempted to take those feelings of loneliness and do something you know is wrong? Did you give in to that temptation?

2. Have you ever known a woman like Potiphar's wife? If she were your friend, how would you counsel her to handle her feelings for Joseph? For her husband?

3. Do you think someone like Potiphar's wife is redeemable? Why or why not? If God can forgive even her, do you believe He can forgive you for whatever you have done wrong? What steps will you take to admit your sins to Him, to allow Him to set you free from whatever bondage you may face right now?

11

Tamar

Futile Words, Broken Promises, Bold Solutions

(BASED ON GENESIS 38)

If I Were Tamar

The sky is darker than usual for this time of day, during this end-of-winter season. I do not mind, really, for the weather matches my mood, and I have been walking in the shadows for so long that to see the sun grates rather than uplifts me as it used to. As it did during the years of my innocence before my first marriage.

I glance down at my widows' garments and wonder if I will ever see color again. My sisters, when I see them, wear the bright colors of women with homes and children, robes that set them apart as blessed—a testament to their husbands' achievements. One even wears the coveted blues of near royalty, for my brother-in-law works in the service of one of the Canaanite kings.

I, on the other hand, am a disgrace to my father's house, a burden he should not have been forced to bear.

"Be grateful your father allows you to return, daughter. You belong in Judah's household while you wait for his son's coming of age. Could the man not have kept you for another year?" My mother's words ring often in my thoughts, as two years have passed and there has been no word from Judah, adding to the gloom that weights my spirits and matches the darkness of my slowly fading hope.

It is hard to imagine that I, still a fairly young maiden of twenty, could have already been widowed twice. Did the gods curse me at my birth? Did Judah's God consider me unworthy? Why then not simply take my life instead of the lives of Judah's two oldest sons—my husbands? Despite the abuse I have suffered under both men, I did not think them deserving of death. I thought, given time, things would change. I could have done better, done more, to please them.

I pick up the basket of linens and head to the river with the soap and hyssop to wash them—a task I used to enjoy with my sisters before they wed, before I wed. Now even my mother prefers to allow me the time alone rather than join me. I have spent too much time alone these past years.

I walk past the forest to the river's edge, barely seeing the familiar surroundings. Judah's firstborn son had seemed like a wonderful choice when my father signed the betrothal agreement for me to marry Er. How handsome he was, how strong and appealing. But his strength was not that of inner character. Er could swing an ax and lift heavy stones, but he could not control his inner urges, and he took his anger out on me from the moment our wedding week had passed.

We were not married long enough for me to conceive a child, and in fact, I think my fear of him kept my womb from fertility. And then came that fateful day when I could not wake him. I shudder at the memory. He had lain with me the night before, but he was not gentle, nor did kind words come from his mouth. I bit my lip to keep from crying out and forced back the tears even after he slept.

I can still hear my own voice screaming his name the next morning. Judah's footfalls had sounded like heavy drums as he'd run to our tent, burst in, and found his son dead. The harshness of his weeping had jarred me, and I realized that grief was the very emotion I should have felt in that moment. But all I could do was stare at my husband's body, stiff and cold on his own pallet. Had he stayed beside me in the night, I might have known sooner, perhaps done something, gone for help.

Judah said that God smote him, and all I could think was, *Which god?* Why would Judah's God take his son?

"He was evil," the gossips said months later at the well when they thought I could not hear. But my sisters had no problem speaking the truth, and I wonder where they got such an idea since it did not come from me. Had Judah's God thought Er was evil?

I kneel by the bank and dip the first garment into the water, its chill rushing through my fingers and adding to the shiver in my soul. Onan had been worse than Er, the way I see it. Judah's second born, my levirate husband, only came to me because his father had commanded it. I knew from the deep scowl on his face that this arrangement did not please him. He wanted to marry his own bride, father children who would inherit Er's portion. But Judah wanted Er's name to be remembered, so Onan entered my tent on the pretext of coming to implant his seed in my womb.

I never understood why he would not fulfill his obligation, why he used me the way he did, purposely preventing me from conceiving. If I had been fearful with Er, I grew angry with Onan.

Had my fear and anger killed both men? I glance at the cloudy sky, gray with the threat of rain. I picked a bad day to wash, but I do not care if I'm caught in a downpour. Let the waters of a wadi wash me away and deliver me from this misery.

I'm told Judah's God killed Onan for his treachery toward me, but with the death of his second son, I'm not certain Judah believed it. He looked at me strangely from that moment on, and once the time of mourning for Onan was past, Judah sent me home to my father.

"I will send for you when my son Shelah is old enough to marry," he'd promised. Most men married between ages eighteen and twenty in our culture, and more than two years had passed since Onan's death. Shelah could have married me six months ago.

I wish my father had never met Judah or his sons. Another man might have loved me, or at the very least been kind to me. I might have enjoyed the company of sisters-in-law by now and held a babe in my arms.

I blink away the stubborn threat of tears and scrub harder on the linen tunic I wear beneath the dark robe of my widowhood. I should have been given to Shelah, as Judah had promised. But I knew when the time passed and no word came from Judah's camp that my father-in-law had no intention of keeping his word.

Why? I look again at the dreary sky, wondering what caused me to seek answers from above. If the God of Judah had taken my husbands and caused Judah to keep me from my rightful place, what had I done to deserve this treatment? I search my heart but can find nothing worthy of this place in which I find myself.

The clothes are washed in short order, and I put them in the basket to carry home. I will dry them there rather than wait hours for them here. I rise on shaky limbs, straighten my back, and walk slowly toward my father's small home. I pass the well, not expecting anyone to be there yet, as it is not time to gather the water for the evening meal. But a small group of women has arrived early, speaking together in animated tones.

Curious, I move closer and greet them.

"Tamar, have you heard?"

I bristle at the way the words are said, as if I should know something I do not. I know so little tucked away in my father's house. "Heard what?"

"They say Judah is traveling to Timnah to shear his sheep," one woman says.

I look at her, my mind muddied. Why should I care what Judah does? He has denied me my right to marry his son. Word has it that he lost his wife the year before Shelah came of age. Perhaps the man was just tired of too much loss, but his neglect of my rights still upsets me when I think on it overmuch.

"Don't you wonder why he is off to celebrate so soon after losing his wife?" another asks.

"He has mourned Bat-shua's death nearly a year, from what I understand," I say, suddenly deciding I want to leave, to run from their questions. "I do not think it wrong for him to shear his sheep."

"Yes, but sheep shearing is a time to rejoice, and from what I understand, men tend to 'rejoice' in sometimes, shall we say, amorous ways." The women all chuckle, as though it is perfectly normal for their men to sleep with prostitutes and temple priestesses whenever they find an excuse to celebrate.

I don't know why such behavior troubles me. It is custom, after all, and these women accept it as easily as the men do. But somehow I cannot imagine Judah engaging in such behavior. He is a Hebrew who follows one God, and his adherence to rules and tradition is strong. He will not sleep with prostitutes.

"Thank you for telling me," I say as I return to the path home. But I cannot forget this information or the women's implications.

Would Judah sleep with a prostitute? And if he does, what is that to me? It is Shelah whom I am meant to wed, to carry on his father's line. To give Er an inheritance in his name. Would a child born to a prostitute take Er's inheritance? But the child would be Judah's, not Er's, for a prostitute had no part in such a covenant.

The thoughts roll around in my head even as I try to sleep that night. All I can think about is Judah's broken promises and futile words. Nothing he's said to me has come to pass. I am forever condemned to wear widows' garments and die lonely and poor in my father's house. I will never be a mother, and no other man will marry me. I am tainted. People view me with suspicion. And Judah has cast me out.

I rise and creep to the window in my father's sitting room and look out on a quiet courtyard. What can I do to change my circumstances? Is there any way to get Judah to keep his word?

In Our World

There was a time in history when people did not lock their doors, a man's word was as good as a written contract, and people had a sense of trust. Perhaps you are thinking, *Seriously? How long ago was that?* Perhaps hearing Joe and Sam's story will better explain how far-reaching is the idea of trust and the words we speak and the oaths or promises we make.

Joe owned a general market in Small Town, Kansas. The store had been in his family for generations, and just like his father before him, Joe was known for extending credit to the local farmers until their crops came in. He even went so far as to help them out when he could during periods of famine or drought.

One customer, Sam, was new to town, and while people tried to be friendly, Sam had a way about him that was not always likable. Joe didn't say so because he was the trusting type, but he felt as though Sam had a sneaky, untrustworthy side to him. Still, Joe believed in giving a man the benefit of the doubt, so he gave Sam the same credit and consideration he did the rest of his customers.

Time passed, and as was typical of the flat farmlands, the rains didn't come one year. Joe had a good living stored up, and his wife agreed that the farmers in the most need should receive the same credit they did when times were good. As you can imagine, everyone loved Joe for his giving spirit and his genuine concern for hurting families.

When the drought ended and a good crop was harvested, his loyal customers paid him in full. All except for Sam.

"I know I said I would pay you," Sam said, "but we've had doctor bills we weren't expecting and the money just isn't there yet. If you would extend the credit a little longer . . ."

The look in Sam's eyes reached the kindness in Joe's heart. "A few more months then," Joe said, and he shook the man's hand.

"I don't trust him," Joe's wife said once Sam left the store. "You wait and see. A few months from now and he'll come around with another excuse."

Joe took his wife's hand and smiled. "I don't trust him either, Lisa, but we have to trust the Lord more. Besides, Sam may yet surprise us."

Months later, however, Lisa's words proved true. Sam delayed keeping his word month after month until Joe nearly forgot the debt. And that was exactly what Sam hoped would happen, because he'd had no intention of keeping his promise. He was exactly as Joe first suspected—sneaky and untrustworthy.

This story might have taken place in the 1800s in Kansas, or it could go back to the 1500s in England, but it really started with the law of Moses. In Numbers 30 we read, "If a man vows a vow to the Lord, or swears an oath to bind himself by a pledge, he shall not break his word. He shall do according to all that proceeds out of his mouth" (v. 2).

I wonder if God had Moses put that law in writing because of men like Judah who preceded Moses and did not keep their word. Or men like Laban who deceived Jacob, or

Jacob who deceived Isaac. Or Sam—my version of Judah fast-forwarded thousands of years.

If you stop to think about it, breaking a promise or not keeping your word is like not telling the truth. And in our day, we do both far too often and much too easily.

Have you been in that place where you listened too often to futile words and empty promises? Have you been told one thing and expected it to happen, and then it didn't? I know I have.

Some people say that if others don't follow through with what they've said, we just need to expect less of them. If we don't expect them to keep their word, we won't be disappointed, right? If Joe never expected Sam to pay him back, he could have just forgiven the debt and let Sam continue to take advantage of him.

In this biblical story, if Tamar never expected Judah to keep his promise for her to marry Shelah, she could have accepted her role as a widow and lived out her life in loneliness. And if she could have forgiven her father-in-law, she might have found some semblance of peace.

But is this really a good way to protect our hearts? While Solomon did tell us, "Keep your heart with all vigilance, for from it flow the springs of life," he followed the admonition with these words: "Put away from you crooked speech, and put devious talk far from you" (Prov. 4:23–24).

It seems Solomon was trying to tell us that our hearts are affected by the words we say and by the words others say to us. Wise words from a wise man, yes?

But this only addresses how *we* might react when others break their promises to us. What about the responsibility they have to keep their word? What about our responsibility to keep ours? Does it really matter in this modern world? After all, we are free to do as we please, and if others don't like it, it's their problem, right?

I've thought on this a lot over the years. Sometimes I've wondered if it is a generational thing. For instance, if you tell my ninety-five-year-old mother that you are coming to take her to dinner at this time on this day, she expects that to happen. It's not that she doesn't understand if someone gets sick and plans are canceled, but barring illness or a snowstorm or some other major reason, she believes your word, as she was raised to do.

But back to the deeper issue here. Should we be expected to keep our word, to fulfill our spoken promises? Is giving our word the same as making a promise, or do we have to say, "I promise"? The truth is, we often make promises, even using words that we know we cannot follow through on.

"I promise I will fix this." But it's a situation we cannot fix.

"I promise I will come back from a dangerous mission." But we cannot know if we will survive it.

"I promise to always be there for you." But we cannot know if tomorrow we will end up in the hospital or be struck with a life-interrupting tragedy.

There are some promises we simply cannot keep and should not make.

Others, as in Judah's case, are a covenant that by law he was obligated to keep. Like Sam in the story above, however, Judah had no intention of keeping his word to send for Tamar when Shelah grew to marriageable age, which some suggest would have been a year or two after her second husband died.

The deceit gene runs through the DNA of each one of us.

Perhaps Judah considered Tamar evil because she was present when both of his oldest sons died. Undoubtedly he feared losing his youngest son as well, and rather than seek God, Judah grew suspicious and sent Tamar away. He broke his word out of fear.

When we break our word today, it isn't out of fear as much as it is selfishly motivated. We change our minds and we don't want to keep our promise, especially when it hurts. Now, there may be a good reason for us to break our word, but can we honestly say that is the norm?

The psalmist asked, "Who may worship in your sanctuary, LORD?" (Ps. 15:1 NLT). He proceeded to answer the question in part by saying,

> Those who lead blameless lives and do what is right,
> speaking the truth from sincere hearts.
> Those who refuse to gossip
> or harm their neighbors
> or speak evil of their friends . . .
> and *keep their promises even when it hurts.*
> (vv. 2–4, emphasis mine)

Judah had already lost so much, and his wife died probably at some point after his second son's death. To give Shelah, his last living son, to Tamar could have cost him deep hurt, something he wasn't willing to risk. And we can almost sympathize with his thinking, can't we?

When we look at our world today, I wonder if any of us is willing to keep our promises if it's going to cost us more than we planned. Politicians make promises they won't keep, and we grow increasingly frustrated and angry because we know that campaign speeches carry empty words.

Even worse is when we hear futile words or empty promises given from a pulpit or in a class, where we come to hear the truth. How many of our leaders in all walks of life are honest, humble, and living their lives with integrity?

Don't get me wrong. I hold leaders in high esteem because on a very small scale I know how hard it is to be in a leadership role. And I've known some truly humble and honest leaders. But leaders are held to a higher standard, and we need to be discerning in whom we listen to and in whom we place our trust. "Wise as serpents and innocent as doves," as Scripture says (Matt. 10:16).

Judah was his clan's leader. He had separated from his family after his bright idea to sell his brother Joseph to the Ishmaelites. And in my opinion, it was probably his guilt that led him to leave his father's camp and marry a Canaanite.

Trouble always begins when we rebel against what we know is right. Judah was living like a prodigal, but he had not forgotten the things his father had taught him. He knew right from wrong. He knew his marriage to the Canaanite went against everything his father, grandfather, and great-grandfather would have wanted. And when his oldest son died, he also knew that the custom of levirate marriage was one he needed to follow. It's when it cost too much that his fear kicked in and he decided he could not keep his word. And Tamar suffered for his broken promises.

We suffer when someone does something as simple as telling us they will call or come over and then they don't. Or worse, when someone breaks a covenant of marriage or a contract we are counting on or a bond of love we expect because we're blood. Broken promises and empty words can litter our lives on every path we take.

If we're honest, it hurts, doesn't it? It hurts to expect something that never happens. It hurts to believe in someone who lets us down. In that respect, I can relate to Tamar. I'm not so sure I would have come to her decision on how to fix things, but she lived in a different century and culture.

Still, I wonder . . . what would you have done?

Imagine with Me

I rub the small of my back after working the millstone, aware of the change in my body. I glance at my mother bent over the garden just outside of the courtyard, plucking the vegetables for the evening meal. A feeling of wonder creeps over me yet again, but I quash the smile that threatens to give away my secret. I need to tell my mother, but I haven't dared. Not yet.

I knew almost the moment Judah had come into me three months ago. My womb had quickened, and a startled sense of awe had filled me, followed by an intense feeling of fear. What had possessed me to play the harlot, to seduce my father-in-law? I was meant for his son, not for him. And in a deeper sense, I felt ashamed of my behavior. I had been almost certain Judah's God would strike me for such an act—dressing up in colorful garments and hiding beneath a shrine prostitute's veil.

My breath hitches at the memory. He had taken no time to ask me to lie with him. I had not been at all certain he would even notice me, but his grief and celibacy had likely fueled his desire. I must admit when I looked in my bronze mirror that my reflection was appealing and could likely entice a man.

Judah was not at all like his sons. It was strange to feel his breath against me, to taste his lips. I closed my eyes, pretending Er had loved me and this was him treating me with such passion and even kindness. Judah didn't rush me or hurt me but treated me with . . . respect. Something I had not expected from the man who had fathered two selfish sons.

When he'd donned his clothes and left, I felt a sense of loss that I could not have had the same treatment from Er. Rather than ponder that thought overlong, I quickly dressed, remembering his promise to send me a goat for my trouble.

But I have no use for a goat. I glance toward my room, where Judah's signet ring and his cord lay hidden at the bottom of a basket of wool. His staff lies beneath the corner of my mat, where I propped extra pillows. Those are the items I will soon need once Judah gets word of my condition.

"Tamar," my mother calls, drawing my thoughts from the child growing within me. I have begun to see a small rise in my middle, and I know the sharp gaze of my mother will soon notice.

I must tell her. My heart hammers at the realization. "I'm here, Mother."

"Come and help me lift this basket." She sits back on her heels, the basket overflowing with cucumbers and leeks and a small melon.

I stand, smooth my widows' garments, and walk toward her. The sun slants at an angle, headed toward its place of evening rest, as I reach her.

She looks at me, her eyes narrow. "You've put on weight, my daughter." She holds my gaze, but I cannot hold hers.

"I've been hungrier of late," I say, hoping she will not press me.

She pushes to her knees, then rises. I lift the basket and we walk toward the house. We work in silence for several moments, sorting the vegetables and setting some aside for the stew and others for the side dishes in which to dip our bread.

"I've noticed," she says softly, looking at me once more. "Is there something you wish to tell me, Tamar?"

I swallow and place a hand on my middle. I look beyond her. "I do not wish to tell anyone," I say hesitantly, "but I am afraid the news will tell itself in a few months' time."

My mother seems to stagger a moment, then finds a seat and lowers herself onto it. She looks me over as if examining me for the first time. "How far along?"

"Three months."

"Whose child?"

"Judah's."

Her eyes widen. "Your father-in-law?"

I nod, tears threatening.

"Does he know?"

I shake my head. "No."

"But he knows he slept with you."

Again I shake my head. "No."

She sits up, suddenly animated. "How on earth could he not know? He promised you to his son. This act is despicable, especially for a Hebrew! Your father will be furious!"

"My father will have no cause, Ima. The blame rests with me." I proceed to tell her how I went to Timnah, where Judah was shearing his sheep, and seduced him. "He thought me a prostitute and I let him think so. He owed me a child, Ima. He was not going to give me to Shelah. I had to do something!" I am crying now, and I realize just how serious is my plight.

"Judah could have you stoned. You have no proof the child is his if he does not even know you deceived him." My mother looks stricken. I have never seen such an expression on her face before, and I am grateful to know how much she loves me.

"I have proof."

She looks up at that, and I lead her to my room and show her my proof. Now if only Judah will accept it once my situation comes to his attention. If he does not, my life and the life of my child will soon end.

From Broken Promises to Restoration

It's hard to wrap our minds around this cultural situation Tamar found herself faced with. The thought of her sleeping with her father-in-law does not conjure positive feelings, nor does the idea of pretending to be a shrine prostitute for the sole purpose of getting pregnant.

She did, however, share feelings we can relate to—feelings of abandonment, of broken promises, of shattered dreams. We've already discussed the fact that the culture of biblical times looked on barrenness or singleness among its women as outside of the norm. Such women, most of the time, would not have lived the lives they'd hoped for.

Sometimes life doesn't match our dreams, and broken promises and empty words can be the catalyst that breaks those dreams. Sometimes other people disappoint us. Sometimes circumstances are beyond our control. Sometimes we realize that our pursuits aren't what we thought they would be.

You could say that Judah was the beginning of Tamar's troubles. If he had stayed in his father's camp and married

188

someone from his family line, he would not have had those three sons and Tamar's story would not be in Scripture. But that was not Judah's journey. And so Tamar's journey is inextricably linked to her father-in-law.

Judah faced a lot of grief for his choices, and he must have exploded with rage when he heard his daughter-in-law had played the harlot. But I wonder if the news of Tamar's pregnancy also brought him the slightest bit of guilt. After all, he had broken his word to give her to Shelah, and he knew it. On the other hand, she had turned her back on his family and slept with another man—just to become pregnant? Whose child did she carry? He would have the man killed if he knew. But Tamar was the one he held the most resentment against. If not for her, Er and Onan might still be alive. She was a curse, a blight, and she deserved to die for this.

The normal sentence for infidelity was death by stoning, but the Bible tells us that Judah demanded she be burned. That's some pretty strong hostility, wouldn't you say?

So Tamar was brought before her father-in-law, her child's father, her judge, and she could probably smell the torches burning and see Judah's servants ready to tie her to a stake and set her ablaze. Good thing she had asked Judah for his staff, cord, and signet—his personal identification papers, so to speak. For when he declared her guilty, she produced her innocence. And in that moment, Judah finally came to his senses, as all prodigals must do, and admitted his hand in her situation. He even declared her more righteous than he was because he had failed to keep his word to her.

Pretty important, a man's word, back then and even today. Though today we toss our words around like they carry no meaning.

Sadly, because we live in a broken world and are born with natures that carry a penchant for rebellion and sin, there will be times when we will be like Judah. We will run from our safety net of family, or we will run from responsibilities that we know are ours. We will say things we don't mean and hurt people we love most. I say this not to judge anyone. I say it because I know it is true of me and of the human race of which I'm a part.

But I also know that Scripture gives us so much hope for broken dreams and promises. For words spoken in haste or with ill intent. It's called forgiveness. When Judah recognized his hand in Tamar's pregnancy, he accepted the truth and acknowledged it before his entire clan. He took Tamar back under his care, though he did not treat her as a wife or sleep with her again. He cared for her and their children (she had twins!) as he should have done all along.

As for Tamar? I wonder what thoughts ran through her mind when at last she was in the home where she belonged. When she held two boys in her arms and realized the dream of motherhood she'd longed for. Did she feel guilt over the way she'd deceived Judah? How did she and Judah explain the children's parentage to them as they grew older?

We can't answer those questions, but we do know that God mercifully looked down on Tamar and allowed her to be included in the lineage of King David and eventually listed in the genealogy of Jesus the Messiah.

Tamar's broken dreams were turned on their head by her bold actions, and while we might not see ours restored as hers were, if we trust God with the outcome of whatever life throws our way, we will find that He can turn broken promises into restored hope.

Ponder this

When we are faced with people in our lives breaking their word to us, or when we have broken our word to them, remember that broken promises can be forgiven. They do not have to define us. And to take it further, God never breaks His word to us. Joshua told the Israelites,

> *Not one of all the L*ORD*'s good promises to Israel failed; every one was fulfilled. (Josh. 21:45 NIV)*

In the New Testament the apostle Paul reminds us,

> *For no matter how many promises God has made, they are "Yes" in Christ. And so through him the "Amen" is spoken by us to the glory of God. (2 Cor. 1:20 NIV)*

Unlike people, God keeps His promises. No matter our circumstances or our frustrations with others or our own behavior, God keeps His word. And He loves us! He will never back out on that.

Taking it further

1. Have you ever experienced the pain of someone's empty words or broken promises to you or someone you love? How did that make you feel? Did you do something to make it right or push it aside and let it go? Did either action on your part bring you peace?

2. Have you ever made a promise with no intention of keeping it? If so, what prompted you to do so? Explain why you believe you were right or wrong in your actions. If you know you've hurt someone by the things you've said and can make it right, are you willing to do so? How do you intend to mend that relationship?

3. Do you think Tamar was justified in her actions with Judah? Do you think she needed to or ever did seek forgiveness from God? How important, in light of this story and of Scripture, do you think it is to mean what we say and keep our word in days to come? Why?

12

Zipporah

When We Wrestle with God

(BASED ON EXODUS 2; 4)

If I Were Zipporah

Our newborn son nestles close to my breast and breathes deeply as his hungry mouth finds sustenance. Gershom. *A sojourner there.* That is the name my husband has given our firstborn. I gaze at his dark hair and tanned skin, thinking the name appropriate for Moses. But not for me. I am not a sojourner. Midian has been home all of my life, my father a respected priest here.

But the Egyptian who is not an Egyptian had come to us a year ago, and my father found him fascinating. Enough so to give me, his eldest daughter, to the man in marriage.

I must admit, I am attracted to the stranger who had walked toward our well with a stick long enough to be a shepherd's staff, but dressed in royal Egyptian robes. What on earth was an Egyptian prince doing in Midian without horse, driver, or chariot? Had he hiked this great distance alone?

By the look of his dusty clothes when he sat on a raised stone near the well, it seemed my deductions were correct. Still, I glanced about me, looking for some sign of another. Surely a retinue would follow. But a prince would not stray from his guards in this barren land. Too many thieves and wild men roam these hills. Even the shepherds who share our wide fields did not treat the daughters of Jethro with kindness. They did their best to drive us away from the well each time we happened upon them when we watered our father's sheep.

But that day Moses had stood up to those men and drove *them* away, then watered our flocks for us! We were all so astonished and uncertain what to say that we simply nodded our thanks and hurried home. I wanted to linger a moment, but I feared if I did the shepherds would return, and I did not know what a band of men would do to Moses, Egyptian royalty or not.

I feel the pull of Gershom's mouth and brush a tendril of thick, soft hair from his face. The memories are still fresh, though over a year has passed. My father had wondered if we had all lost our senses for not having offered the man food and lodging, and I felt ashamed that as the eldest I had not thought of it.

A sigh escapes, and I settle into the joy of nursing my son. Moments later, footsteps sound with the telltale thump of a shepherd's staff. Moses pokes his head into the tent where

I rest. He smiles and I return the gesture. I cannot say that I love this man I call husband, for even after a year of sharing his tent I do not know him. Not really. He has told my father the reason for his flight from Egypt, and my father has welcomed him. But even in the privacy of our tent, Moses does not share his past with me other than to say that he is both Egyptian and Hebrew. And once I told him I had conceived, he informed me—he did not ask—that if it were a boy he would be named and circumcised on the eighth day after his birth, in accordance with the covenant of his Hebrew heritage.

"He is hungry today," Moses says, his gaze now on our son.

"He is always hungry." I cannot help the smile, for nursing this child brings great delight. I do not admit how exhausted the feedings have made me.

"You are resting enough?" His comments and questions are never long, and sometimes I want to drag words from him.

I nod, though my silent admission is a lie.

"And he has healed well?" He means from the circumcision.

I stare at my husband, forcing back the anger that still bubbles to the surface at what he insisted must be done, which caused our child such pain. I will never forget his pitiful cries as long as I live. Pray God if I ever bear another child it will be a girl!

Moses waits for me to answer, his patience another reason for my annoyance. He seems forever patient, hesitant even, and I wonder how a man can be so even-tempered, especially when I know he has fled here for his life. Is there no anger in him toward those who hunted him? No fear?

"He has healed." I say the words through clenched teeth. Later, when I am stronger, I will make my feelings known to my husband. For now, he has informed me that I am to rest for a month or more until I have become well accustomed to motherhood.

"Good," he says, taking a step away from the door. "I will come back when I return with the sheep." He slips away, and in the distance I can hear him calling the sheep by name. He had never shepherded before coming here, he'd said, but he is a quick learner. My father allowed him the care of the flock and set my sisters to doing other tasks.

A sense of sorrow fills me with his leaving, and though I look long into Gershom's dark eyes, I feel a sudden weariness sweep over me. I should feel grateful that Moses came along and made me a mother. Other men in the nearby towns had never been of much interest to me, and I will admit Moses intrigues me. He no longer dresses as an Egyptian, and with time his beard has filled in and he fits in better with our people.

But his heart is so often far away. Though he was not raised among his Hebrew people—he's told me that much—he does know of their covenants, and he feels an inner compulsion to keep the ways of their God. I understand obedience to a god, as my father is highly religious. He knows of this Yahweh of which Moses speaks.

But for a covenant to cause my son to bleed and cry out in pain—and at such a young age? The anger that lives within me surprises me at its strength, for by now I thought I would have healed along with my child. Yet time has simply made me see that I will not be so passive the next time. I will stand up to Moses. I will argue my case and defend my child should I be blessed with another son.

Gershom might bear the symbol of Moses's covenant people, but any other son born to him will not! I will make sure of it.

In Our World

Have you wondered if marriage has ever been easy? A wild new adventure into an exciting new life? If you look back at the Victorian era or the ancient worlds of Greece, Rome, Egypt, or the Bible times of which I write, wouldn't you think there might be some examples of marriages that never faced a single problem? (I hear you laughing!)

If you are married or have ever been married, you probably find the thought of a problem-free life, let alone a problem-free marriage, ridiculous and impossible. And you would be right, because we are a fallen, wounded, baggage-bearing people.

We see things differently than our spouse does, no matter how much we have in common. Then add in the different ways the sexes think. Let's face it, no matter who we are, how much money we make, or how perfect the other person seemed before we said "I do," we find out soon enough that we did not enter utopia. Sometimes we've entered a battleground.

Lisa did not realize the emotional baggage Brian had carried into their marriage until their first fight. His words were harsh, accusing, and, if she didn't know better, abusive. So she apologized for whatever it was she had done, even though she didn't understand what that was. Had she said something wrong? Done something he didn't like? But Brian didn't come out and tell her specifics. Perhaps he'd just had a bad day.

Johan picked Cyndi up from her job at the library, expecting to enjoy a quiet evening with his smiling bride. But Cyndi was not smiling when she fairly flopped into the seat and tossed her purse into the back. Johan tensed, waiting for a barrage of complaints that had become all too common of late. He could understand if the complaints caused Cyndi real emotional harm, but they were always petty. He never knew when things would be terrible or wonderful. There seemed to be no middle ground with her anymore. Had there ever been?

He listened with one ear as he drove and searched his mind, trying to understand when Cyndi had begun to change. Surely she had not acted this way before the wedding, had she? But a dark side of her, a side that changed with the wind, had come over her as soon as the honeymoon ended. He had tried asking her to seek counseling, but every attempt at such a suggestion was shot down with a cold look and a slammed bedroom door.

These examples are but a few of the many struggles you may encounter when you marry. Perhaps your spouse had an abusive father, and the only way he knows how to react is in anger. Or perhaps that abusive father made him passive-aggressive, and you have trouble communicating because he seems to go along with you but won't admit what is really brewing inside.

Another often overlooked aspect of marriage is what is going on inside of a spouse emotionally and spiritually. Cyndi in the above example was bipolar, but she functioned well when things were going her way, as in before the wedding. But after many months of marriage, Johan began to see a side of Cyndi that he didn't recognize, and it scared him. One minute she was shouting at him incoherently, while the next day she was everything sweet. Johan felt as though he was walking on eggshells in his own home.

Sex outside of marriage and living together before marriage are other behaviors that people don't realize take an emotional toll. Guilt, shame, and regret are only a few of the emotions you might feel, because when you give your body to another, you are bonding with that person. While some may say we want sexual freedom, sex isn't free.

Sex with the husband or wife of another person is also dangerous territory. Solomon referred to it this way:

> Can a man scoop fire into his lap
> without his clothes being burned?
> Can a man walk on hot coals
> without his feet being scorched?
> So is he who sleeps with another man's wife;
> no one who touches her will go unpunished.
> (Prov. 6:27–29)

Sex outside the bonds of marriage can touch our lives in ways we don't expect, and it can have far-reaching effects.

Then there are those who marry inside the church, like Mary and Levi, but Mary doesn't realize that Levi is not truly a believer. This is complicated, and I've seen it in different scenarios. Sometimes the would-be spouse becomes a "believer" in order to win the hand of the beloved, but that faith never transforms their character, and though they go to church and do all the right things, their heart is not changed.

Or take the case of Will, who marries Kari, a good church-going girl. They live happily together for years, but deep inside she cannot make herself share his faith on the level he lives it. She wrestles with emotions about God and eternity until one day, when their first child grows gravely ill, she is forced to face them. Kari cannot discuss the matter with Will. She's too ashamed to admit that maybe she's not the good Christian girl he thinks her to be. But at last she confides in a friend who speaks truth to her, and Kari prays like never before. She believes at last . . . but she's lived a lie for seven years and needs to tell Will the truth. He takes it well—with joy, in fact—but a nagging part of him doubts himself. How could she have deceived him? How did he not know?

Like I said, marriage is not without its trials and struggles.

We get it, don't we? Perhaps we can look at Zipporah differently now. The truth is, the Bible says very little about her. In fact, she is only mentioned three times, and commentaries struggle to make sense of one passage where she circumcises her son. I've pondered it in an attempt to understand it myself. On the surface, it is confusing. And I'm not saying that I have some back channel to understanding Scripture or that my imaginative interpretation is correct.

But when I look at human nature and marriage and their culture, I have to wonder about Zipporah's character. I've shown her to be protective of her child and angry about a religious rite that caused her son pain—for reasons she did not understand or necessarily agree with. She was a Midianite, after all, not a Hebrew. She did not share the covenant promises of God that Moses did. So if Moses circumcised his firstborn, as he knew God had commanded, it makes sense to me why Zipporah knew what to do many years later when she took a completely different course.

Imagine with Me

"Please let me go back to my brothers in Egypt to see whether they are still alive." Moses speaks the words to my father one evening.

I look up from my spinning in a corner of my father's house. I'm enjoying those few moments I have with the men after the evening meal, before it is time to put the boys to bed. Is he serious?

I set the spindle aside and take each of my sons by the hand. We head to the door, but not before I level a look at Moses. *And when were you going to tell me this news?* We have been at odds since Eliezer's birth, and he is now five and has been weaned for two years. Our strife continues because I had refused to allow Moses to circumcise this son. If God was truly his help and had delivered him from the sword of Pharaoh, as Eliezer's name implies, then why go back to the place from which he'd been freed?

"Go in peace."

I hear the words come from my father's mouth, but I had expected better from him. An argument, some sort of pleading. But no. My father trusts Moses's God, and if God has spoken to Moses, then he must obey.

I am not so easily convinced. But the next morning we saddle a donkey with both boys in tow and head down the hill, away from all that is familiar to me. From Midian. To go to a land I do not know and a people who might not accept my sons or me. What will happen if they reject us? Worse, what will happen if God doesn't help Moses and protect us all? We could lose our sons.

I listen to the thump of Moses's staff as I walk beside the donkey, my heart yearning to turn back, my mind willing my feet to move forward. I cannot leave my husband. My father would not wish to care for my sons and me while Moses goes off on this fool's journey.

And I do not wish to leave this man who is both strange and appealing to me. I feel almost shame when I think on the one argument we have had, where he gave in to me with resignation. Would his God truly expect him to circumcise every son? After what we put Gershom through, surely Moses can understand how I feel.

"I don't want Eliezer to bear this mark of your covenant," I'd said the day after his birth. "Name him now and we will move on with our lives. There is no need for a ceremony. It is not like we worship this God of yours. We do not sacrifice to Him or worship in His temple."

"He has no temple. He needs no temple," Moses said. "And I do not build altars for sacrifice because I do not know how. I was raised Egyptian, remember?"

"You know enough to know about this covenant." I spat the words and then regretted my outburst at the wince he gave. I had wounded him at some level. Is it because he misses the years he could have lived with his true parents? Does he wish he had not been saved by the princess he calls Mother?

Why these memories surface now as we trudge away from my father's camp, I do not know, but I cannot deny them or the regret that accompanies them. I never apologized, for to do so would mean I am willing to give in, to change my mind, and the older Eliezer grows, the less I am willing to subject him to that ritual.

We walk for hours, and as the sun begins to set, Moses picks a place to lodge for the night. We have just finished raising the tent when I see a man approaching Moses, his face hidden but his intent all too clear. My heart hammers and bile rises up the back of my throat. The man catches Moses's arm and tosses him like a child to the ground. He kneels over my husband, his arm raised, a flint knife in hand.

A flint knife. A common weapon men carry. The same tool Moses used to circumcise Gershom. Moses struggles beneath the weight of the man, but he at last stills as though he is simply waiting for the stronger, bigger man to cut his throat.

God, where are You? My mind screams the words, and in a flash the man turns deep-set eyes on me. I feel stripped of everything I hold dear, my emotions making my whole body quake. But I know. I know exactly why this man holds my husband's life in his hands.

It's my fault. The words reverberate in my head as I grab a flint knife from Moses's pack and take Eliezer's hand. "Lie down," I command, and in an instant, I lift his tunic and cut off his foreskin. Eliezer screams, then bursts into quiet tears, likely for fear of the man as well as the pain.

I stride with purpose toward them both and cast the foreskin at Moses's feet. "Surely you are a bridegroom of blood to me!"

The man stands and lowers the flint knife. He stays a moment longer to look from Moses to me, making me see that I am indeed the cause. I had refused to let Moses keep the covenant, and now Eliezer will be unable to travel as quickly. How much simpler would it have been if I had not argued but done as God required when Eliezer was an infant?

Why? my mind cries out, but my lips are silenced at the look of gentle rebuke and love all bound up in a moment of time. And then He is gone.

I stare at the place where He had been, then meet Moses's gaze. "A bridegroom of blood," I say again. All because of the circumcision that I will never understand.

From Fighting to Freedom

We have examples in Scripture of Jacob wrestling with God, Job arguing with God, Jonah whining and complaining to

God, Thomas doubting God, David disobeying God, Solomon thinking himself wiser than God, and on and on. In a sense, Zipporah fought with God. What may have started with an arranged marriage to a man she did not know ended with her faced with a God she did not know and could not see, but it became alarmingly clear to her that He was not to be mocked or disobeyed.

I rather doubt that Zipporah realized that this strange God chose her husband for a very important and dangerous mission. In her mind, she probably expected to live out her days with a fugitive Egyptian Hebrew in a shepherding town in the hills of Midian. But when God steps into a life, everything changes and we are not the same, guaranteed.

Moses didn't want this call on his life. He argued with God and tried to wiggle his way out of leading Israel out of Egypt. He didn't want to go back there, and he didn't want to face Pharaoh. And he had no idea whether his own people would welcome him.

So we have Moses arguing with God, and Zipporah, in a sense, wrestling with God's plan. I say "wrestling" because if she was the cause of her son not being circumcised, then she was flexing her will against that of her husband's God. The reason it seems more likely that Zipporah had a hand in this denial of the covenant is because it was *she* who finally gave in and did the circumcision to save her husband's life. Had Moses obeyed the covenant, he would have completed the ritual, not his wife. Either way, they had both disobeyed something God considered important.

Zipporah recognized that truth at a critical moment and did what pleased God. And maybe, in what seems like a split-second scene in Scripture, a radical change occurred in her heart as well. Could it be that she wrestled with God, even competed with God, because Moses was not all she wanted him to be? His background, his hesitance, even his fear, had changed him over time. And when he finally submitted to God's plan to go back to Egypt, Zipporah probably sensed she had lost him to his God and his people.

That's where I think her marriage to Moses changed. Following this incident in Exodus 4, we hear no more of Zipporah until Exodus 18 when her father brings her and her sons back to Moses, after he had finally succeeded in bringing the Israelites away from their oppressors.

I wonder how Moses and Zipporah parted. After her bitter-sounding words where she called him a bridegroom of blood, did they reconcile? Did he thank her for saving his life or remain silent while she felt guilty that his near death was her fault? Did he speak sweet words of comfort to her before he sent her on the donkey back to her father? We cannot know—at least not in this life. Perhaps someday God will give us insight into these unrecorded details.

In any case, Zipporah strikes me as a strong woman. We don't know where she fell in the line of Jethro's seven daughters, but since other places in Scripture indicate that marrying from the oldest to the youngest was the custom of the day, it makes sense to think that she was his firstborn. Firstborns tend to be leaders. And she was quick to respond when she circumcised her son and saved her husband's life.

So perhaps living with the humble Moses (for that is how God saw him years later) drove her a little crazy. Strong-willed people don't always get along with humble people. And the whole circumcision thing—somebody opposed it for one or both children, and based on Zipporah's comment, my guess is that it wasn't Moses.

Perhaps she'd been at odds with him over this and other things throughout their marriage. Like I said before, marriage isn't easy, and there is no marriage on earth that is perfect and without struggle.

Yet in the end, Zipporah returned to Moses and apparently lived with him until her death. Some think Moses had a second wife from Cush, but other commentaries believe Midian was close enough to Cush that this wife was Zipporah. Either way, we hope at some point she found a way to live among the Hebrew people and love the man who was also a friend of God. Somewhere along the way, I hope Zipporah learned to trust her husband's God. Whether she fought against Moses or God, wrestled with herself or with God, we don't know for certain. But as with anyone who lives with turmoil in their marriage, I hope she found peace and freedom.

Marriage, at its most spiritual, godly level, has the potential to grow more peaceful and loving and sacrificial as we focus on God and not on ourselves. But it takes two willing people to surrender our strong wills or fearful wills to trust His ways, His winding roads, and His call on our lives. Doing so can bring us together in a better harmony than we might have known in the beginning.

Just like Zipporah and Moses separated for a time and perhaps fought over the covenant, disobeyed, and even argued with God, there will be times in our marriages or in our single lives when we may do the same. As humans we tend to fight before we give in. We want our way above God's way because we think we know better. We think ourselves wiser, better, stronger than God. I know. I've had my share of wrestling matches with Him over one issue or another. And it often takes hardship or a new challenge to make me finally face the fact that He was right all along.

Can I let you in on a secret? God always wins. Moses and Zipporah might have preferred their comfortable hillside shepherd town to separate lives and Moses's call to be a great deliverer. But God called, and He didn't take no for an answer.

———

Brian did not want to listen to Lisa and sit through counseling sessions to help him deal with his abusive tendencies. But he didn't want to end up like his father, and deep down he knew God wanted to heal him. So he swallowed his pride and went.

Cyndi could not believe that anyone would accuse her of mental illness. That's all she could think of when the doctor said *bipolar*. But Johan loved her enough to keep insisting they go together to counseling and find the right medication to help, and they realized that lots of people suffer from these kinds of maladies. This was no different than if Cyndi had had a physical ailment such as diabetes. Mental illness is a disease in a different part of our bodies. Once Cyndi realized that, she wanted help and received it.

It probably seems like this chapter is all about marriage, but it's really about realizing that we live in a broken world and we all bring our past with us into new relationships. Most of us don't like being told how to live, so like Zipporah, we fight, we compete, we wrestle with the change. At our deepest level we grapple with God's will.

God wants the absolute best for us, and despite our tendencies to be like many of the women in this book—those of us who blow it big-time like Eve, who try to fix it on our own like Sarai, who try to put our will up against God's like Zipporah—we will find that we really don't know best. We can't always fix things. We can't get out of this broken world. We can't undo it, change it, redo it, or do anything to make it better except one thing. Give our broken pieces, our sins, our struggles, our messes, to God, who is the only one big enough and strong enough and wise enough to make all things new.

And one day He will. We can be part of that new beginning if we simply ask Him to take our lives, just as they are, and turn them into the lives He wants them to be. He wants us to trust Him with our dreams, even when life isn't going at all the way we'd planned. He can turn those dreams into something even better than we can possibly imagine and give us joy in the journey on this adventure we call living.

But it takes our willing hearts to get to that place. We can be offered His greatest gifts, but they won't be ours unless we accept them. Won't you reach out and place your hand in His today? Stop fighting His will for your life and accept His plan. I promise you really will discover that He knows best, and His best is glorious.

Ponder this

When we are faced with things in life that we just don't understand, when our relationships face struggles, when our way of doing things does not match what God requires, remember that God is not out to cause us pain. He has set guidelines and made promises for a reason.

We know that in all things God works for the good of those who love him, who have been called according to his purpose. (Rom. 8:28 NIV)

Even those things that don't seem good right now, God is using for our good. If we love God, we can count on this promise. He is taking those very trials and making them into something better than we could ask for or imagine. He will work even the greatest trial for our good if we love Him. Count on it.

Taking it further

1. Have you ever felt like someone you loved wanted God more than they wanted you? How did that make you feel? Did you feel as though you were in competition with God? Did that person truly love God, or did they use Him as a means to control you?

2. Why do you think marriage to a man like Moses might have been difficult, especially for someone like Zipporah? How would you have handled Zipporah's situation when she found herself up against a covenant she didn't understand? Do you ever feel that way about things in God's Word?

3. Do you ever find yourself wrestling with God over things you know He wants you to do? How does that make you feel? What steps can you take to accept His plan?

Conclusion

When I was young, I had a lot of dreams and expectations of what life should look like. Some of what I envisioned came true. Some of it didn't. Much of the time, God has taken me down paths I would not have chosen. You see, I have this tendency to think I know best. I wonder how many of us can relate to that thinking.

We can choose the path we want to follow. God allows us that ability. If He had not made us with the ability to choose, we would be like the animals that roam the earth. They do not stop to think before they seek shelter from prey or just play in the sunshine. They do so instinctively.

We, on the other hand, are not animals. We are human beings made in the image of the living God. And because He gave us choice . . . well, we want to be autonomous and live our lives our way. No one enjoys being told what to do. The trouble is, eventually we will run smack-dab against a sovereign God whose choice outweighs and outrules all others. If we want to tangle with God, we are not going to win. And even if He lets us have our way, at some point in the future—even if it's at the end of our days—we are going to wish we'd made a different choice.

So what do we do with those dreams for the life we want to build for ourselves? And if we want what God wants and still see our dreams die, what then? How do we trust God when everything we hoped for or expected is shattered?

These are hard questions, and I don't have brilliant answers for them. Honestly, my life feels rather shattered as I write this, and it has for many years in one way or another. Sometimes I wonder if I have a breaking point. When your heart feels like it's as fragile as glass, and that glass falls and breaks and the splinters cover the path right where you're walking, what then?

On our honeymoon over forty years ago, we bought a blown-glass carousel. It sat in a display case on a glass shelf for years and years. One day, when I finally decided to dust the neglected room where it sat, I found that the glass shelf had somehow fallen and the carousel with it. I was glad that only some of the base had broken, but those twisted glass pieces are impossible for me to fix. They need a professional glassblower to mend them. I can't even hold the pieces in place long enough or well enough to glue them.

That's what happens to us when we face a life that doesn't match our dreams. We thought we would grow up and become something that just didn't come true. Maybe we are thwarted by injury, or the competition is too great, or we end up in a dead-end job just to pay the bills and can't afford to do the thing we longed to do our entire lives.

Or maybe poor health prevents us from fulfilling our desires. Infertility has ruined many a couple's dreams of family. Cancer has cut short the joy of family. As the stories in this book show, there are many reasons why life doesn't match our dreams.

But maybe the journey we are facing does not mean God is saying, "No, this will never happen." Maybe the reason we have not yet realized our dreams is because we took a wrong turn in the path, or God is saying, "Not yet. Wait." And in the waiting, "Trust Me."

I've never ever liked to wait. (True confession: patience is my Achilles' heel.) But waiting is exactly what God has often asked me to do. And I've come to see that waiting is married to trust, and the two together birth hope. That's why we need to take a deep breath, step back, and hold out open hands to our loving God.

He doesn't withhold the fulfillment of our dreams to hurt us. Sometimes He delays our dreams to teach us to trust Him. We trust Him by surrendering those dreams into His care. We pray for what we want, and we pray for Him to choose what's best for us. We might have to let our dreams die, but like a seed planted in the ground, whatever we give up to God has the potential to grow into an amazingly impossible dream far greater than we could have ever asked for or imagined.

The question is, are we willing to let God determine our way and give us the desires He wants us to have? Are we willing to surrender our dreams into His care and wait for Him?

I'm still learning to do this. My prayer for each of you is that you will join me on this journey. Let's all learn to trust God together with what we long to see but can't control. After all, He loves us most and He knows us best. And that is reason enough to trust Him.

Acknowledgments

In 2016, I sat across the table at a restaurant in California and chatted with my agent, Wendy Lawton, about the possibility of writing a nonfiction book. I had sent Wendy a basic idea, and we discussed it more over lunch. I never dreamed she would find the idea exciting or that Revell would take the risk of moving me (temporarily) from fiction to nonfiction. The segue from one to the other wasn't that difficult because my focus is still on women of the Old Testament. Nevertheless, this has not been an easy book to write, and I have Wendy and my friend Hannah Alexander to thank for pre-reading the book when I was certain I was making a mess of it all!

As always, my gratitude toward everyone on each team at Revell is never ending and grows with each new book. Thank you to all—Lonnie Hull DuPont and Jessica English, my fabulous editors; Jennifer Nutter, my marketing manager; Melissa Anschutz, my publicist; and Gayle Raymer, my cover designer.

To Randy, you are my best friend. I'm so glad God has allowed us to do life together. To my family, you know how much I love you—always and forever.

Most importantly, thank you, Yeshua Messiah, for allowing these women to be immortalized in Scripture. Knowing even part of their journeys helps us to know we are not alone.

Jill Eileen Smith is the bestselling, award-winning author of the Wives of King David, the Daughters of the Promised Land, the Wives of the Patriarchs, and the Loves of King Solomon series. Her research has taken her from the Bible to Israel, and she particularly enjoys learning how women lived in Old Testament times.

When she isn't writing, she loves to spend time with her family and friends, read stories that take her away, ride her bike to the park, snag date nights with her hubby, try out new restaurants, or play with her lovable, "helpful" cat, Tiger. Jill lives with her family in southeast Michigan.

Contact Jill through email (jill@jilleileensmith.com), her website (www.jilleileensmith.com), Facebook (www.face book.com/jilleileensmith), Twitter (www.twitter.com/Jill EileenSmith), Instagram (www.instagram.com/jilleileen smith), or Pinterest (www.pinterest.com/JillEileenSmith).

Meet
JILL EILEEN SMITH

at **www.JillEileenSmith.com** to learn interesting facts and read her blog!

Connect with her on

Jill Eileen Smith

JillEileenSmith

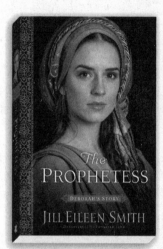

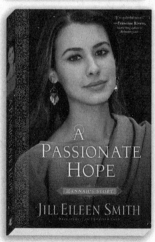
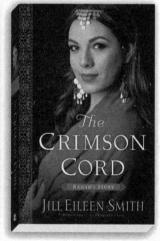